From the Deep Woods to Civilization

Dr. Charles Alexander Eastman, Ohiyesa

The Lakeside Classics

FROM THE DEEP WOODS
TO CIVILIZATION

Including excerpts from
Indian Boyhood

By
Charles Alexander Eastman

EDITED BY
A. LaVonne Brown Ruoff

The Lakeside Press

R.R. DONNELLEY & SONS COMPANY
CHICAGO
December, 2001

PUBLISHERS' PREFACE

As we write this Preface, terror has struck from the air in New York City and Washington, D.C. Although it is difficult to contemplate "business as usual," we believe it is important to return to our normal activities so America and the world can reclaim their sense of stability and security.

We are relieved to report that all our employees who worked a block from the World Trade Center are safe. We applaud the bravery of rescue workers in New York and Washington, and the generosity exhibited by so many in the immediate aftermath of this tragedy. Right now we are in mourning, but we look forward to a time of healing and to a renewed sense of purpose. The pride and spirit of the American people, and our recognition of the importance of our freedoms, will undoubtedly be the enduring remembrance of 11 September 2001.

This is the ninety-ninth year of The Lakeside Classics. Some of those years suffered great wars, others experienced peace; years of economic uncertainty have been balanced by decades of great prosperity; sadness has been tempered by the exhilaration of accomplishment.

The Lakeside Classics has published many books about the exploration and settlement of North America by European peoples. These have, perforce, described the interaction between native and western

European cultures. But very few of these accounts have been from the viewpoint of the American Indian. *From the Deep Woods to Civilization,* the autobiography of Charles Alexander Eastman, a Santee Dakota (Sioux), attempts to provide that perspective.

Born in 1858 near the site of the modern city of Minneapolis, Minnesota, Eastman lived in a time and place characterized by rapid change. Government treaties, military actions, and white migration into the Dakotas forced the Sioux to resist or to adapt. Either way, they lost land and much of their tribal culture.

In this book Eastman relates his transformation from a traditional Native American youth to a westernized, highly educated professional adult. At the urging of his father, he began this journey at a school for American Indians in the Dakota Territory. After attending Beloit and Knox Colleges in preparation, he moved on to Dartmouth and then to Boston Medical College, where he became one of the first American Indian physicians. He was assigned to the Pine Ridge Agency as the first native physician in the Indian Bureau's service. A highlight of the book is Eastman's description of rescue efforts to locate Indian casualties following the battle of Wounded Knee. After leaving his medical career, he continued to serve his people as a spokesman, author, and organizer.

* * * *

Thomas E. Donnelley, son of the company's founder, introduced The Lakeside Classics series in 1903. T.E.

believed that a well-designed and expertly manufactured book would be an appropriate gift from a company that prided itself on high-quality products and services. We continue to honor T.E.'s original concept, employing the latest commercial techniques to manufacture the book.

Our historical editor for this year's edition was A. LaVonne Brown Ruoff, professor emerita of English at the University of Illinois at Chicago, where she developed the Native American Studies program, and former interim director of the D'Arcy McNickle Center for American Indian History, The Newberry Library. Ruoff has directed four National Endowment for the Humanities Summer Seminars for College Teachers on American Indian Literature and received a Writer of the Year award for Annotation/Bibliography from the Wordcraft Circle of Native Writers and Storytellers. She is currently editor of the American Indian Lives series of the University of Nebraska Press.

* * * *

Charles Alexander Eastman eventually found personal fulfillment when he learned how to combine the best of his traditional Native American culture with the ideals of Western civilization. In many ways, R.R. Donnelley is experiencing a similar journey. We are growing into a world-class communication-solutions company by building on our heritage—as a leading provider of printing—and by adding services to meet the diverse demands of a changing world.

Like Eastman, we have found that transformation can be challenging. We embrace our traditions, while we develop ways to integrate and adopt new processes and technology. This journey is made somewhat easier because some things do not change. Our values remain the same: leadership through the pursuit of excellence; respect for all, integrity always; one team committed to common goals; customer intimacy and insight; leading change through innovation.

We are working steadfastly to align our culture with our business strategy and organizational structure. Emphasizing our values, we have implemented new initiatives to strengthen how those values are modeled in the daily workplace.

Last year in this Preface, we introduced three investment strategies to focus our efforts and grow our business. This year we made significant progress on developing our business models and leveraging the enterprise to achieve distinct advantage in the market.

In our print business this led to a decision to restructure, enabling our marketing and sales organization to focus on designing print solutions for targeted customer segments. Our manufacturing teams are fine-tuning our operations and building a more customer-responsive and flexible print platform. The new print structure is called R.R. Donnelley Print Solutions. Several programs are key to the success of this new structure, including Continuous Improvement, which jump-starts quality, cycle time, and customer service; Business Process Redesign, which standardizes, streamlines, and integrates manufacturing processes; and significant capital equipment upgrades. We are working toward the industry's most flexible, robust, and efficient processes—larger plants that are better located and better equipped.

Strategic and significant capital investments were made in existing plants at Mattoon, Illinois; Glasgow, Kentucky; and Lancaster, Pennsylvania. Consolidation resulted in several plant closings: St. Petersburg and South Daytona, Florida, and Houston, Texas, Financial Printing. We also announced the closing next year of the Des Moines, Iowa, and Old Saybrook, Connecticut, facilities.

As we evaluated our investments in premedia, logistics, direct mail, healthcare and financial communications, Internet services, and certain international markets, we identified customers' requirements and began to transform those businesses. For example, to provide more effective four-color directories in international markets, we opened three new facilities. Flaxby Moor, England, which opened in June, is the most technologically sophisticated directory printing facility in the world. It serves customers from the United Kingdom, continental Europe, the Middle East, and Africa. The business and employees from the now-shuttered York Telecom plant were transferred to Flaxby Moor.

Flaxby Moor uses line-of-sight manufacturing, with operations configured in a straight line. This design is serving as the model for our new Shanghai facility, scheduled for groundbreaking late this year. The plant will meet the varying needs of a developing print environment. We also opened a second plant in Kraków, Poland, to expand capacity for our customers on the European continent that require telecommunications, magazine, and catalog work.

We proudly and confidently face our markets, our employees, and our investors as an organization that is transforming itself to provide more comprehensive, better-integrated communication services.

* * * *

We would like to thank George A. Lorch, who retired in July from our Board of Directors after five years of service. We welcome Gregory Q. Brown and Norman H. Wesley to our Board. Mr. Brown serves as chairman and CEO of Micromuse, Inc., which is a provider of network diagnostics and quality-assurance software. Mr. Wesley is chairman and CEO of Fortune Brands, Inc., an international consumer products holding company.

To our employees, retirees, customers, suppliers, and friends, we express our hope that the new year will bring renewed security, peace, and happiness.

THE PUBLISHERS

December 2001

CONTENTS

PART I
Excerpts from *Indian Boyhood*

PART II
From the Deep Woods to Civilization

xiv   *Contents*

ILLUSTRATIONS & MAPS

HISTORICAL INTRODUCTION

Cʜᴀʀʟᴇs Alexander Eastman's *Indian Boyhood* (1902) and *From the Deep Woods to Civilization* (1916) are among the most important American Indian autobiographies published in the early twentieth century. Together, they trace Eastman's life from boyhood as a traditional Dakota through his transformation into a physician, popular author, and internationally known lecturer.

Eastman's chronicles are important because they record the radical changes in American Indian tribal life after a series of government actions and white migration onto tribal lands. The passage of the Indian Removal Bill of 1830 forced Indian tribes east of the Mississippi to move to Indian Territory (now Oklahoma) and other locations. The westward movement of settlers onto Indian lands, resettlement of Indian tribes onto reservations in the 1880s, and the passage of the General Allotment Act (1887), which assigned tribal land to individual Indian males, altered the American Indian way of life. During his lifetime, Eastman's own Santee Dakota nation and the Lakota nation, among whose people he later worked, endured tremendous changes.

Indian Boyhood and *From the Deep Woods to Civilization* combine elements of the Euro-American literary and Native American oral traditions, even though the European concept of a formal history of a whole life or autobiography was not part of American Indian storytelling tradition. In many traditional Indian societies, telling one's life story would be considered inappropriate and egotistical. To do so would set that person apart from the group, thereby threatening the harmony of the community.

In the oral tradition, however, there were many ways in which individual acts of bravery or of cowardice could be told. A camp crier or storyteller might relate tales of courageous acts, men might exchange stories around a campfire, or a warrior might describe in a speech his own victories in battle to demonstrate that he had achieved the status necessary to speak on a given issue.

At the close of the nineteenth century, as Indians were coerced onto reservations or into Indian Territory, non-Indians grew more interested in reading about the "vanishing Americans." Consequently, personal narratives of Native Americans gained considerable popularity. The life history that evolved in this period spans both oral and written literatures, incorporating elements of oral storytelling and personal statement, as well as written autobiography.

* * * *

To offer a picture of the life and times of Charles Eastman, from his Dakota childhood through his acculturation and, finally, disenchantment with assimilation into white society, this edition of The Lakeside Classics combines excerpts from *Indian*

Boyhood with the full text of *From the Deep Woods to Civilization.*

Indian Boyhood, originally written for Eastman's children, is a fascinating description of growing up Dakota. The book appeared in more than twenty editions, some in foreign languages. A hundred years after it first appeared, it is still in print and widely read. *Indian Boyhood* is a vivid and moving account of Eastman's childhood as a traditional Dakota. The book chronicles Eastman's experiences from birth to his reunion at age fifteen with his father.

In these excerpts, Eastman does not describe his life in strict chronology. Instead, he divides the narrative into important events and into the seasonal cycle of Dakota life, which he exemplifies with incidents from his experience. He creates a strong portrait of his loving and heroic grandmother, Uncheedah. Charming stories about making sugar in sugar camp, playing boyhood games, shooting his tiny arrows at a full-grown moose, gathering foods like wild rice and roots are balanced with tales of threats to Dakota safety and survival.

Although Eastman beautifully describes the plentiful harvest of wild rice and roots, he also emphasizes that hunger was an ever-present danger. Boys may play their boyhood games and his tribe may celebrate winning a lacrosse match, for example, but the Dakota must be ever alert to attack from the Ojibwa, prepared to go to war against the Gros Ventre, or ready to protect their ponies from being stolen by the Blackfeet.

While young Hakadah (Eastman's Dakota name) begins to learn at age three how to hunt, he also experiences the hard lessons of Dakota rituals. One of the most dramatic episodes occurs when Uncheedah uses her moral authority to persuade her eight-year-old grandson to sacrifice his most beloved possession, his dog. Like the good Dakota grandmother she is, Uncheedah gently helps him reach this conclusion himself. To avoid offending his non-Indian readers, Eastman does not reveal that the sacrificed dog probably would have been cooked and eaten as part of the ritual.[1]

While *Indian Boyhood* celebrates the traditional Dakota at the end of the nineteenth century, *From the Deep Woods to Civilization* chronicles Eastman's move from that life to Euro-American culture. In form, this volume is similar to conventional autobiographies of the period. It depicts how the author overcame the obstacles of moving from being a well-trained and respected Dakota to becoming a well-educated, successful, and acculturated member of American society.

From the Deep Woods to Civilization falls into three major sections. The first describes Eastman's encounters with the non-Indian world from age fifteen until he graduates from medical school. But his path was not smooth.

Even at the outset, his father and grandmother dis-

---

[1] According to the Reverend Samuel Pond, the sacrificial dog could sometimes be tied with a stone and thrown into a lake as an offering. See "The Dakotas or Sioux in Minnesota as They Were in 1834," *Minnesota Historical Society* (1905-08), 12.

agreed about the direction that his life was to take. Uncheedah eloquently sums up traditional world views of the Dakota: "The Great Mystery cannot make a mistake. I say it is against our religion to change the customs that have been practiced by our people ages back." His father, however, ends the discussion with a firm statement that persuades his son and silences Uncheedah: "Here is one Sioux who will sacrifice everything to win the wisdom of the white man! We have now entered upon this life, and there is no going back." This becomes Eastman's credo as he follows the hard, lonely path to acculturation and assimilation.

Eastman attended schools far from his Dakota friends and the tribal culture that had nurtured him. He describes both his determination to become acculturated and his sense of strangeness. He reveals his ambivalence about his experiences at Dartmouth: "It was here that I had most of my savage gentleness and native refinement knocked out of me. I do not complain, for I know I gained more than their equivalent." He greatly expanded his intellectual interests and met many influential people during his years at Dartmouth and Boston Medical College (later Boston University School of Medicine). At the same time, he remained an outsider among his non-Indian acquaintances.

The second major section of the autobiography describes Eastman's experiences as he attempted to establish a career. Particularly significant is the section on his work as a government doctor to the Pine Ridge

Lakota. He offers vivid portrayals of Lakota leaders, detailed descriptions of the impact of the Ghost Dance on the Lakota, and a moving account of the horrors of the Wounded Knee massacre.

Later, he describes his disillusionment with corrupt Indian agents at Pine Ridge and politicians in Washington. Disappointed in the "character of the United States Army and the honor of government officials," Eastman nevertheless argues that he had "seen the better side of civilization."

The third section focuses on Eastman's growing sense of his own Indian background and heritage and his final statement on his philosophy. His many trips to Indian reservations and visits with his family and friends in Canada rekindled his connections with traditional Indians. He describes his joy at a particular visit, during which he feasted and exchanged stories with family and friends and also visited his grandmother's grave. The depth of his need to connect with traditional Indian people and the deep woods is revealed when he meets with some Ojibwa, the Dakota's ancient enemies. Spending time in nature revitalized a demoralized Eastman. He confesses that "every day it became harder for me to leave the woods." The renewal he felt during this period enables him to reach the philosophical positions he states at the very end of the book.

* * * *

As did other Indian and African American authors in the nineteenth and early twentieth centuries, Eastman authenticates his narrative by numerous references to people who befriended him and notable people he met. One of the challenges early Native American and African American narrators faced when they wrote their life histories was how to get their audiences to believe the truth of their stories. By including testimonials from or numerous references to prominent people, these authors preempted any charge that they did not write their life histories or that their accounts of what they endured were untrue.

Most American Indian life histories were narrated to translators or collaborators. One of the earliest and most popular of these was *Black Hawk, an Autobiography* (1833).[2] Black Hawk told his life story in his Sac language, Antoine LeClaire translated it into French, and John B. Patterson rendered the French into English.

As Indians became educated in English and in Euro-American literary traditions, they began to write autobiographies, which often combined oral history, myths and tales, and personal experience. The first American Indian autobiography to be published was *A Son of the Forest* (1829) by William Apess (Pequot, b. 1798). It chronicles the experiences of a five-year-old boy taken from his abusive grandparents and hired out to a series of harsh masters. The book appeared during the debate over the issue of Indian removal from the Southeast and Midwest.

[2] *Life of Black Hawk* was published in 1916 as the fourteenth book in The Lakeside Classics series.

An early Native American autobiography that dealt extensively with traditional Indian culture, blending myth, tribal history, and personal experience is *The Life, History, and Travels of Kah-ge-ga-gah-bowh* (1847) by George Copway (Ojibwa, 1818-69), expanded as *The Life, Letters, and Speeches of Kah-ge-ga-gah-bowh* (1850). Copway wrote the book during the period when the government was trying to remove the Ojibwa from ceded territory to central Minnesota. Raised as a traditional Ojibwa from Rice Lake, Ontario, Copway converted to Methodism, was sent to Illinois for nineteen months of formal schooling, and became a missionary in Wisconsin, Minnesota, and Rice Lake. He later became a lecturer and author in the United States.

Life Among the Piutes: Their Wrongs and Claims (1883), written by Sarah Winnemucca (Paiute, ca. 1844-91), is the first book-length personal and tribal history by an Indian woman. She provides an incisive and detailed account of Paiute customs, as well as a hard-hitting attack on corrupt government officials. Like Eastman, these early autobiographers were public lecturers.

Eastman was not the only Plains Indian to write an autobiography in the early twentieth century. Standing Bear (Ota K'te) (Oglala Lakota, ca. 1868-1939), Eastman's contemporary, published *My Indian Boyhood* (1931). He is best known for his *My People, the Sioux* (1928), a powerful account of his journey to and experience at Carlisle Indian School, and *Land of the*

Spotted Eagle (1933), which focuses on Sioux beliefs, customs, and life. Gertrude Simmons Bonnin (Zitkala-Ša) (Yankton Dakota, 1876-1938) published autobiographical essays in *The Atlantic Monthly* in 1900 and 1901, which were reprinted in her *American Indian Stories* (1921). These essays contain moving accounts of growing up as a Dakota girl, surviving harsh treatment at a Quaker boarding school in Indiana, attending Earlham College, and teaching at Carlisle.

Another Plains Indian description of the boarding experience is *The Middle Five* (1900) by Francis La Flesche (Zhogaxe) (Omaha, 1857-1932), which appeared two years before Eastman's *Indian Boyhood*. This delightful book portrays a group of Indian boys at a Presbyterian mission school in northeastern Nebraska.

* * * *

Eastman traveled a long way from the traditional lives of his parents, both of whom were descendants of generations of leaders of the Wahpeton and Mdewakanton bands of the Santee Dakota.

Eastman's maternal great-grandfather was Mahpiya Wicasta or Wichasta (Cloud Man, b. 1780), a Mdewakanton chief who had a French father and Mdewakanton mother. Cloud Man was one of the earliest converts to Christianity. His daughter, Eastman's maternal grandmother, Wakinajinwin (Stands Sacred), married Seth Eastman (1809-75) at Fort Snelling in 1830, the year Charles Eastman's mother was born.

Charles Eastman's maternal grandfather, Seth Eastman, was from New Hampshire. He graduated from
West Point and became both a topographical engineer
and celebrated painter while serving as a U.S. Army
officer. He left his Indian family behind in 1833, when
the War Department reassigned him to Louisiana. In
1841, he returned as commander of Fort Snelling,
accompanied by his white wife, Mary Henderson
Eastman (1818-87). She later wrote *Dahcotah: or Life
and Legends of the Sioux Around Fort Snelling* (1849)
and other books on Indians.

Charles Eastman's father was named Ite Wakanhdi
Ota (Many Lightnings, 1809-75), a Wahpeton whose
father and grandfathers had been chiefs. Eastman's
mother was Wakantankawin (1830-58), which he
translates into "demigoddess" in the book *Indian
Boyhood* (according to anthropologist Beatrice Medicine [Dakota], the terms "Holy Woman" or "Sacred
Woman" are more accurate translations). Her English
name was Mary Nancy Eastman.

Many Lightnings and Wakantankawin married in
1847 and had three sons and a daughter before
Charles Eastman[3] was born in February 1858, near
Redwood Falls, Minnesota. He was named Hakadah
(The Pitiful Last). His mother died in either July or

---

[3] Biographical information about Charles Eastman is taken
from the following sources: David R. Miller, "Charles Alexander
Eastman, The 'Winner': From Deep Woods to Civilization, Santee Sioux, 1858-1939," *American Indian Intellectuals*, ed. Margot
Liberty (Saint Paul, MN: West, 1978), 61-73; Raymond Wilson,

Seth Eastman, Charles Eastman's
maternal grandfather, in U.S.
Army uniform, ca. 1860

Many Lightnings
(Jacob Eastman),
Charles Eastman's father

From the Deep Woods to Civilization

September 1858; accounts vary. The paternal grandmother, Uncheedah, was chosen to rear the baby and
raised Eastman to age fifteen. Living far from contact
with whites, Hakadah was raised to be a traditional
Santee Dakota.

The name "Hakadah" was changed to "Ohiyesa"
when, after winning a lacrosse game in 1862, his band
renamed the four-year-old boy Ohiyesa (The Winner). For the rest of his life, even after he adopted the
English name of Charles Eastman, he continued to
use this name.

After the 1862 Dakota Uprising in Minnesota,
which started when the Santee attacked the Lower
Sioux Agency and ended with the defeat of the Santee
at the Battle of Wood Lake, the government severely
punished the rebellious Santee Dakota, and Eastman's father was imprisoned. His grandmother and
uncle, with Ohiyesa in their care, joined other Santee
fleeing first to Dakota Territory and then, in 1864, to
Manitoba, Canada. During his three-year imprison-
ment, Eastman's father, Many Lightnings, converted
to Christianity and took the name Jacob Eastman. Released, he settled in 1869 near Flandreau, Dakota Territory, and then traveled to Canada to find his son.

———

"Charles A. Eastman (Ohiyesa)," *Native American Writers in the United States,* ed. Kenneth M. Roemer, *Dictionary of Literary Bi-ography* (Detroit, Washington, D.C.: Bruccoli Clark Layman/Gale Research, 1997), 175: 75-83; and Wilson, *Ohiyesa: Charles East-man, Santee Sioux* (Urbana: University of Illinois Press, 1983).

Because he felt that Indians must adapt to white ways, Jacob insisted that his son return to Flandreau with him, and then he persuaded Ohiyesa to convert to Christianity. As part of his conversion, young Ohiyesa selected the names "Charles" and "Alexander" from a book of names he borrowed from a minister.

As part of his acculturation, and despite Uncheedah's strong objections, Jacob enrolled Charles in the Flandreau mission school, which he attended for two years. Charles then walked some 150 miles to enter Santee Normal Training School, at Santee Agency in Nebraska, where his brother John worked as a teacher. After Eastman had completed two years at Santee Normal, the Reverend Alfred Riggs, his mentor, obtained government aid for Eastman to study in the preparatory program at Beloit College, Wisconsin, 1876 to 1879, and at Knox College in Illinois, from 1879 to 1881.

Although he returned to Flandreau to clerk in his brother-in-law's store and then accepted a temporary teaching position at a local mission school, Eastman's higher education was not finished. Riggs helped his protégé gain a scholarship to Dartmouth College, whose original charter was to serve American Indians. He traveled to Dartmouth in 1882, but first attended Kimball Union Academy, a preparatory school, for eighteen months in 1882-83. He entered Dartmouth in the fall of 1883 and graduated in 1887.

Friends such as Frank Wood, a Boston printer and activist in Indian affairs, assisted Eastman in obtaining

Charles Eastman, 1876

funds for him to enter Boston Medical College in 1887, from which he graduated in 1890. Charles Alexander Eastman thus became one of the first American Indian doctors.

Eastman then returned to his roots. He began his medical career in November 1890 as the physician at the Pine Ridge Agency, in present-day South Dakota. Shortly thereafter, he met Elaine Goodale (1863-1953),[4] who would become his wife in June 1891. Goodale was of New England stock—her ancestors landed at Salem, Massachusetts, in 1632. Educated at Sky Farm, her home in the Berkshires of western Massachusetts, Goodale was precocious. She and her sister Dora wrote and published their poetry in journals and received enthusiastic praise. This encouraged them to publish their collected poems in *Apple Blossoms: Verses of Two Children* (1878), which sold more than 10,000 copies and brought them acclaim in the United States and England.

Her career took a very different direction after Gen. Samuel Chapman Armstrong visited Sky Farm in 1878. Armstrong was the founder and head of Hampton Normal and Agricultural Institute, Virginia, which

[4] Biographical information on Elaine Goodale Eastman has been taken from the following sources: Ruth A. Alexander, "Elaine Goodale Eastman and the Failure of the Feminist Protestant Ethic," *Great Plains Quarterly 8* (Spring 1988), 89-101; Elaine Goodale Eastman, *Sister to the Sioux: The Memoirs of Elaine Goodale Eastman, 1885-91*, ed. Kay Graber (Lincoln: University of Nebraska Press, 1978; written in the 1930s); Raymond Wilson, *Ohiyesa: Charles Eastman, Santee Sioux.*

had been established primarily to educate freed slaves after the Civil War. Greatly impressed by Goodale, Armstrong offered her a position in Hampton's American Indian Department. She accepted the position in 1883 and became a much-beloved teacher of Sioux students, who taught her their language, as well as an effective public relations writer for Hampton. After Goodale toured the Great Sioux Reservation in 1884, she resolved to devote herself to educating Sioux children. The following year, she opened a school on the west bank of the Missouri River at the mouth of the White River. In 1890, she became the first supervisor of Indian education in the two Dakotas.

Soon after they were introduced in 1890, Elaine Goodale and Charles Eastman became engaged. In the midst of their courtship, they were caught up in the events surrounding the Seventh Cavalry's massacre on 29 December 1890 of Big Foot's band of Miniconjou at Wounded Knee Creek. Both helped to care for those caught in the fighting or fleeing from it.

After the hostilities subsided, the couple traveled to New York City, where they married in a lavish ceremony on 18 June 1891. In her memoir *Sister to the Sioux*, Elaine Goodale Eastman describes her promise to marry Eastman as a "two-fold consecration": "I gave myself wholly in that hour to the traditional duties of wife and mother, abruptly relinquishing all thought of an independent career for the making of a home. At the same time, I embraced with a new and deeper zeal the conception of life-long service to my husband's people. How simple it all seemed to me then—how far from simple has been the event."

Their first child, Dora Winona, was born in 1892. The Eastman family eventually included five more children: Virginia, Irene, Eleanor, Florence, and Ohiyesa II (Charles Alexander).

But, by early 1893, Eastman's disputes with authorities over government policies became so intense that he resigned his position and moved his family to St. Paul. Although he passed the Minnesota medical board examination, he was unsuccessful in establishing a medical practice.

Thus began a series of short-lived projects, jobs, and other activities, many of which required extensive travel. In 1894, he became Indian secretary of the International Committee of the YMCA. During his first ten months on this job, he was frequently away from home, visiting all the associations on Sioux reservations in South Dakota, North Dakota, and Nebraska. Among his achievements were the establishment of annual Indian workshops in the summer to train leaders and the development of new Indian YMCA groups among the Sioux.

In the 1890s, Eastman and his brother John represented the Santee in their claims against the government dating back to the events following the 1862 Uprising. In 1863, Congress passed an act abrogating all previous treaties with the Santee; this enabled the government to cease paying annuities to the tribe. The Santee wanted to revisit this issue. Unfortunately,

Elaine Goodale, at about seventeen years of age, 1880

Charles Eastman with his first child, Dora

Charles Alexander Eastman II, Ohiyesa II, 1903

From the Deep Woods to Civilization

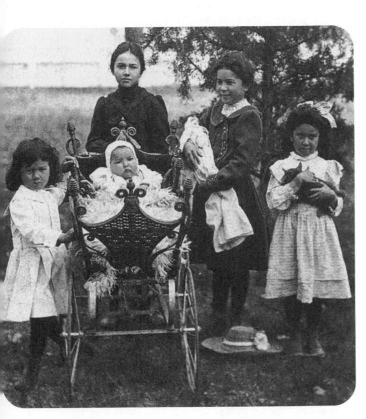

The Eastman daughters, outside their home in Amherst, Massachusetts

questions about who should represent the tribe resulted in a split into two factions, one headed by the
Eastmans and the other by James Garvey, a mixed-
blood clergyman and former teacher at Santee Normal
Training School.

Then, in 1896, the Santees signed a contract with
Eastman and Charles Hill, a former Indian agent to
the Santee, which was approved by the secretary of
the interior in 1897. Controversies over this contract,
the issue of who actually represented the Santee, and
appropriate attorneys' fees lasted for twenty years.
Eastman's attempts to persuade other tribes to hire
him as a legal representative were unsuccessful.

In 1899, Eastman became an agent for a program
that enabled Carlisle Indian School (Pennsylvania)
students to work on white-owned farms during the
summer. Eastman traveled to reservations to recruit
Indian students and supervised the program. In 1900,
Eastman accepted his second post as a reservation
physician, this time at the Crow Creek Reservation in
present-day South Dakota. As he had at Pine Ridge,
he attempted to bring good health care and medical
facilities to the Indians and whites he served.

But, once more, Eastman became embroiled in
controversy with reservation and government officials,
who made unsubstantiated charges against him.
Reservation agents, who wielded almost absolute
power during this period, undoubtedly resented this
educated Indian physician who could communicate
fluently with his fellow Sioux. Eastman's difficulties

with officials at Crow Creek (and earlier at Pine Ridge) grew out of the injustices he saw or experienced. Officials also resented his and his wife's ability to plead his case to influential people in the government and in the organizations supporting Indian causes.

One of his more enduring contributions began in the spring of 1903, when Eastman accepted the job of revising the Sioux allotment rolls for the United States government. The General Allotment Act of 1887, which allotted tribal land to individual male Indians, made accurate rolls a necessity. Eastman revised the names of almost 25,000 Sioux to provide them with consistent surnames that would not embarrass them and that non-Indians could easily understand. As much as possible he retained the original meanings of the Indian names.

After he left this job in 1909, Eastman primarily earned his living as a writer and lecturer. A year later, he traveled to northern Minnesota and Ontario to collect native artifacts for the University of Pennsylvania Museum. Meeting the tribal leaders of his ancient enemies, the Ojibwa, trading stories with them, hunting and fishing, and spending time in nature revitalized a demoralized Eastman. That year he also began his long association with the Boy Scouts of America. He talked to Scout groups, aided camp directors, and served as a national councilman. In addition, Eastman contributed articles for their magazine, *Boys' Life*, and wrote *Indian Scout Talks* (1914), which became a guide for both the Boy Scouts and the Campfire Girls of America.

His involvement in the outdoors movement and his family's need for a steady income undoubtedly convinced the Eastmans to establish their own summer camp in 1915. Originally called School of the Woods, it was located at Granite Lake, New Hampshire. In 1916, it was expanded by creating Camp Oahe for girls and Camp Ohiyesa for boys. The whole Eastman family worked at the camp, which became a major source of their income.

From 1910 to 1920, Eastman continued his work with organizations that promoted greater understanding of Indians. In July 1911, he proudly served as the North American Indian representative at the First Universal Races Congress, which promoted interracial harmony and world peace, held in London, England.

The same year, Eastman participated in the creation of the American Indian Association, whose name was later changed to the Society of American Indians. While serving as its president in 1918, he campaigned for Indian citizenship and against the Bureau of American Indian Affairs, which he felt should be abolished. (The association/society flourished in the 1920s but no longer exists; the Bureau of Indian Affairs continues under the Department of the Interior.)

This peripatetic existence took a toll on his marriage. Over the years, the Eastmans grew apart. Continuing financial problems, different cultures and backgrounds, and Eastman's frequent absences as he pursued various projects created tensions that escalated after the death of their daughter Irene in 1918. Three years later the couple separated. They never discussed the reason for their separation, which they did not publicly acknowledge, and their extant correspondence contains no references to it.

Perhaps their different views of the benefits of assimilation contributed to their breakup. Eastman favored a more selective form of assimilation rather than the uncompromising full assimilation his wife supported. Clearly, he was moving toward reclaiming his Sioux heritage, while Goodale Eastman identified with her own New England ancestry.

Their married life had not been easy for either of them, as she makes clear in *Sister to the Sioux*: "That first little home built for us, the center of so many loving hopes, was sorrowfully abandoned within two years for what proved to be a series of dubious experiments. Unforeseen complications led to repeated changes of occupation and of scene.

"He traveled widely, even to London, and met hosts of interesting people. I was inevitably housebound. But I had always something of a one-track mind, and for many a year every early dream and ambition was wholly subordinated to the business of helping my talented husband express himself and interpret his people."

She also emphasizes that for ten years, she "carried the more burdensome responsibilities of a summer camp for girls in New Hampshire—a job undertaken when past fifty with the help of my older girls and for their benefit. . . ."

For the next eighteen years, from about 1921 through 1939, Charles Eastman spent most of the winter months in the Detroit area close to his son, Ohiyesa II. During that period, from 1923 to 1925, Eastman once more served in the Indian Service as an inspector, conducting inspections of conditions and problems, and investigating charges against Indians and government employees.

He then returned to the lecture platform in the late 1920s and, in 1924, traveled to the city of Chicago, where he saw for the first time Frank Blackwell Mayer's drawing of his mother, which is in the Ayer Collection of the Newberry Library (see color photography section for this illustration).

By 1927, Eastman had become a director of the Brooks-Bryce Foundation, which promoted better relations between English-speaking people in America and Great Britain. He also made speeches for the organization and, in 1928, represented it on a two-month lecture tour in England. After his return he built a bungalow, called Matotee Lodge, on the north shore of Lake Huron, near Desbarats, Ontario, Canada. Eastman's daughters and his grandchildren visited him there. The Indian Council Fire, a Chicago organization of Indians and non-Indians, gave him its first Indian Achievement Award at the Indian Day celebration on 22 September 1933. The ceremonies were held at the Century of Progress exposition at the Chicago World's Fair.

After a tepee in which he had been living caught fire, Eastman suffered smoke inhalation, complicated by pneumonia and by a heart condition. He died on 8 January 1939. Eastman, who had lived to be nearly eighty-one, was buried in Evergreen Cemetery in Detroit, Michigan. The grave was unmarked until 1984 when Raymond Wilson, Eastman's biographer, and the Dartmouth Club of Detroit erected a monument.

Following Goodale Eastman's separation from her husband, she lived with her daughters in Amherst and Northampton, Massachusetts. She continued her writing career, although none of her books were as successful as those she and Eastman wrote together. Goodale Eastman died in 1953 at age ninety and was buried in Northampton, Massachusetts.

* * * *

The Eastmans worked together on the books issued under his name. Goodale Eastman described the collaboration: "Dr. Eastman's book left his hand . . . as a rough draft in pencil, on scratch paper." From these she typed copies, "revising, omitting, and rewriting as necessary" (as quoted in Wilson, *Ohiyesa* 130). Goodale Eastman comments in *Sister to the Sioux* that she urged her husband to write down his "recollections of the wild life, which I carefully edited and placed with *St. Nicholas: An Illustrated Magazine for Young Folks.* From this small beginning grew *Indian*

Boyhood and eight other books of Indian lore, upon all of which I collaborated more or less." After the family moved to St. Paul in 1893, Eastman began to record his childhood experiences, which were serialized in six installments in *St. Nicholas* (between December 1893 and May 1894).

The popularity of *Indian Boyhood* inspired the Eastmans to write three collections with reinterpretations of legends and their own fiction. *Red Hunters and the Animal People* (1904) combined myths with adventure and animal stories based on observations of Indian hunters. *Old Indian Days* (1907), one of the first collections of short fiction to be published by a Native American author, portrayed the life and customs of the Santee Dakota in Minnesota and the Dakota from the early eighteenth century through the 1860s. In 1909, they published *Wigwam Evenings: Sioux Folktales Retold,* a delightful collection of traditional stories.

Eastman also wrote several books of nonfiction. *The Soul of the Indian* (1911) continues to be widely read as a guide to understanding Indian religion, interpreted from a Sioux perspective. *The Indian To-day* (1915) surveys Indian history, Native Americans' contributions to the United States, their achievements, and reservation life. In 1916, Eastman published the second volume of his autobiography, *From the Deep Woods to Civilization.* His discussion of Sioux history in this volume led him to write one of his best works, *Indian Heroes and Great Chieftains* (1918), which is an important source of information about these leaders. After separating from his wife, Eastman wrote no more books.

In her own right, Goodale Eastman was a prolific writer on Indian issues, as well as a novelist, poet, biographer, and playwright. Her earliest works of fiction are *Little Brother o' Dreams* (1910) and *Yellow Star: A Story of East and West* (1911), which she termed "potboilers." She also interpreted tribal myths in *Indian Legends Retold* (1919). Her more mature novels are *The Luck of Old Acres* (1928) and *One Hundred Maples* (1935), her best work of fiction. *Sister to the Sioux* (1978), written in the 1930s and published posthumously, is a memoir of her life among the Sioux from 1885 to 1891. *Pratt, the Red Man's Moses*, is her biography of Col. Richard H. Pratt, who advocated policies of assimilation.

* * * *

Essential to appreciating Eastman's comments on Indian-white relations is an understanding of the complexity of his task in writing his autobiography. Like nineteenth-century American Indian autobiographers and slave narrators, Eastman attempts to describe what his people have suffered without alienating his readers. The criticisms of some contemporary readers, that Eastman was not sufficiently militant in his reactions, ignore the strength of some of his comments, as well as public sentiment in 1916.

In *From the Deep Woods to Civilization*, Eastman

harshly condemns how the government deprived the
Lakota of much-needed rations. He also forcefully
describes the aftermath of the massacre at Wounded
Knee when members of Big Foot's band were
"relentlessly hunted down and slaughtered while
fleeing for their lives." Later, Eastman tempers his reactions to avoid antagonizing his audience. Ac-
knowledging that the tragedy at Wounded Knee
deeply tested his faith in "the Christian love and lofty
ideals of the white man," he concludes, "Yet I passed
no hasty judgment and was thankful that I might be
of some service and relieve even a small part of the
suffering."

That Eastman had cause to worry about the reactions of non-Indians is clear from two reviews published in 1916. *The Literary Digest* huffed that "A
racial—perhaps it would be more accurate to say a
tribal—strain of morbidness, which reveals itself at intervals in all his writing, is somewhat tiresomely obvi-
ous in this latest effort." The *Springfield Republican*
dismissed the significance of the book as a personal
narrative, saying "It is of interest in showing the effect
of education of Christianity on a mind alien to both,
but is almost wholly a narrative of personal affairs,
which are of small importance, and has little social or
educational value."

Far more insightful was the review in *The New York
Times*: "Interesting in part for the light it throws on
the treatment of Indians by the United States government, but far more interesting as the record of one

who honestly sought to appropriate the white man's civilization as the highest good." Generations of readers would echo these sentiments.

* * * *

Eastman lived in a period that saw great upheaval in the lives of American Indians—where they lived, with whom they lived, how they lived.

During the mid- and late-nineteenth century, the Santee Dakota consisted of the Mdewakanton (People of Spirit Lake), the Wahpeton (Dwellers Among the Leaves), Wahpekute (Shooters Among the Leaves), and Sisseton (People of the Swamp).[5] (See Notes on American Indian Nations section, which follows this Historical Introduction.) But the encroachment of white settlement into traditional Santee Dakota territory in southern Minnesota brought pressure from the federal government for the tribe to move westward.

Consequently, the Santee signed the Treaty of 1837, the Treaty of Traverse des Sioux, and the Treaty of

[5] For an overview of both the Santee Dakota and Lakota, see "Sioux (Dakota, Lakota) Indians," *The New Encyclopedia of the American West,* ed. Howard R. Lamar (New Haven: Yale University Press, 1998). For other sources on the Santee Dakota, see Gary Clayton Anderson, *Kinsmen of Another Kind: Dakota-White Relations in the Upper Mississippi Valley, 1650-1862* (St. Paul: Minnesota Historical Society Press, 1997); Anderson, *Little Crow: Spokesman for the Sioux* (St. Paul: Minnesota Historical Society Press, 1986); Roy W. Meyer, *History of the Santee Sioux: United States Indian Policy on Trial* (Lincoln: University of Nebraska Press, 1967).

Mendota (the latter two in 1851). Under these treaties, the Santee relinquished claims to much of their land in Minnesota in exchange for resettlement on reservations along the upper Minnesota River, above New Ulm in southwestern Minnesota and extending to Stone Lake, 140 miles north. In 1858, they ceded to the government a ten-mile strip north of the Minnesota River.

One of the negotiators of this treaty was Little Crow (Taoyateduta, ca. 1810-63), chief of the Kapozha or Kaposia band of Mdewakanton. But by 1862, the Santee nation was furious with the government because annuity payments had been delayed. The Santee were feuding as well with traders over whether the annuities for the 1858 settlement paid all Indians' debts or only those incurred prior to the agreement. Congress then fueled their anger by not passing the legislation necessary to house and feed the Santee. The tribe also deeply resented white settlement on what the Dakota regarded as their hunting grounds.

Hostilities broke out on 17 August 1862, when several Indians, primarily from Rice Creek Village, killed six whites. The Indians then reported their actions to the Rice Creek members of the lodge. Once the group agreed to declare war, warriors marched to the house of Little Crow. In *Old Indian Days* (1907), Eastman says that Little Crow seized "his opportunity to show once and for all to the disaffected that he had no love for the white man." Scholar Gary Clayton Anderson, however, concludes in his *Little Crow* (1986) that few men were dragged more reluctantly into war. The day

*Little Crow, chief of the Kaposia band of Mdewakanton,
who led the Uprising of 1862*

Courtesy Minnesota Historical Society

Little Crow's wife and children at Fort Snelling prison camp

Courtesy Minnesota Historical Society

after the meeting at Rice Creek, Little Crow and his warriors attacked the Lower Sioux Agency. The conflict ended on 23 September 1862, when Little Crow's warriors were defeated in the Battle of Wood Lake.

The Santee suffered severe reprisals for their participation in the uprising. A military tribunal tried nearly 400 full- and mixed-blood Santee and sentenced 303, including Eastman's father, Many Lightnings, to be hanged. President Abraham Lincoln pardoned all but forty. One had his sentence commuted on recommendation of the military commission that tried him, and, at the last minute, the name of one more was removed from the list of condemned. On 26 December 1862, in Mankato, Minnesota, the remaining thirty-eight were hanged as a group, while the assembled crowd cheered. Other warriors, like Many Lightnings, were imprisoned.

Punishment continued when the Congress also stopped annuity payments to the tribe. Because of strong pressure from whites, the government removed the Santee from Minnesota, regardless of whether or not they participated in the uprising. Over the years, some returned; others, like Eastman's relatives, fled to Canada. By November 1863, the Santee straggled into Fort Garry (now Winnipeg), Manitoba, where they begged and sold their children for food. More than 3,000 arrived in the Red River Métis Settlement by spring 1864. Under treaties signed in 1867, most of the Santee were removed to the Santee Reservation in Nebraska, the Sisseton Reservation in South Dakota, or the Devils Lake Reservation in North Dakota. (For further information about the various groups of Sioux, as well as other tribes located in this region, see Notes on American Indian Nations following the Introduction.)

Earlier, in the 1840s, tensions between Lakota[6] and non-Indians greatly increased as well, as growing numbers of non-Indians migrated to Lakota territory. To protect the settlers, the federal government added to its military presence along the Platte River.

In 1851, the United States government coerced some of the Teton Lakota chiefs into signing the first Treaty of Fort Laramie, known also as the Treaty of Horse Creek. In return for the Lakota agreement to remain peaceful and avoid certain areas, the government promised annuities. From 1864 through 1868, the Lakota and the U.S. military fought sporadically. Lakota resistance was strengthened by news of the 1862 Uprising in Minnesota, the 1864 massacre of peaceful Cheyenne by Colorado militia at Sand Creek, and the increasing white incursions on Lakota territory.

Between 1868 and 1876, the government tried to persuade the Lakota to adopt a white lifestyle and to

[6] For information about the Lakota, see especially Robert W. Larson, *Red Cloud: Warrior-Statesman of the Lakota Sioux* (Norman: University of Oklahoma Press, 1997); Catherine Price, *The Oglala People, 1841-1879: A Political History* (Lincoln: University of Nebraska Press, 1996); Robert M. Utley, *The Lance and the Shield: The Life and Times of Sitting Bull* (New York: Holt, 1993); and Utley, *The Last Days of the Sioux Nation* (New Haven: Yale University Press, 1966).

move permanently to agencies on or near their reservations. After the discovery of gold in the Black Hills, white miners rushed into the area, adding to the tension. In 1876, the government sent troops to force the Lakota to relocate.

In the summer of that year, a large number of Lakota, Cheyenne, and Arapaho gathered with Sitting Bull, chief of the Hunkpapa Lakota, in Montana at the Greasy Grass River, known to non-Indians as the Little Bighorn. On 25 June, Crazy Horse, the Hunkpapa war leader, and at least 2,500 well-armed warriors, most of whom were Cheyenne, fought Lt. Col. George Custer and his 211-man command of the Seventh Cavalry. The killing of Custer and most of his men in this battle was as disastrous for the Lakota as the 1862 Uprising had been for the Dakota. Hostilities ended in 1877 after the starving Lakota surrendered. Crazy Horse continued to fight but finally surrendered in May 1877. Later that year he was arrested; when he tried to resist, he was killed by a soldier.

However, the Lakota who followed Sitting Bull into Canada did not give up until 1881. Claiming that the Lakota had broken the second Fort Laramie Treaty, which had been signed in 1868, the United States seized the Black Hills.

Meanwhile during the 1880s, the Great Sioux Reservation had been divided into five separate reservations: Standing Rock, Cheyenne River, Lower Brulé, Rosebud, and Pine Ridge. By 1890, conditions on these reservations were intolerable. Corrupt agents and inadequate food supplies brought the Lakota to near-starvation. The government distributed to the Lakota only about half the food it sent the army.

By the summer of 1890, the messianic Ghost Dance religion, founded by Wovoka, or Jack Wilson (Paiute), brought hope to many of the dispirited Lakota. Its message of peace in a world without whites, and of reunion with dead ancestors who had returned to earth, had great appeal.

In an attempt to stamp out this religion, the Pine Ridge Indian agent had Sitting Bull arrested. The revered leader was killed in the process on 12 December 1890. The government then sent the Seventh Cavalry to pursue Big Foot and his band of Miniconjou, mainly consisting of old men, women, and children. On 29 December 1890, at Wounded Knee Creek in present-day South Dakota, white soldiers massacred 146 Lakota men, women, and children who were then buried at a mass grave at the site. Several wounded died shortly thereafter, increasing the number to 153. Because many wounded Indians escaped and probably died later, estimates of the total number of dead range as high as 300. Charles Eastman was the physician at Pine Ridge Reservation, just miles from the site of Wounded Knee. His first-person account of the aftermath of this tragedy is profoundly moving.

* * * *

Essential to understanding Eastman's philosophy and acculturation is his belief in what he calls a "Christian civilization." Most Indians at this time were educated either in missionary schools or in those with a strong religious influence, and Indian agents and missionaries strongly urged Indians to convert. One of the appeals of Christianity for Indians was that its doctrines seemed to offer equality with whites, even though reality did not match this ideal. Throughout *From the Deep Woods to Civilization*, Eastman stresses his belief in a Christian civilization, which he describes as "the broad brotherhood of mankind, the blending of all languages, and the gathering of all races under one religious faith."

At the end of the autobiography, Eastman advocates civilization both because Indians can no longer live their former life and because the "white man's religion is not responsible for his mistakes." Eastman's concluding statement makes clear that although he has learned much from civilization, he has "never lost my Indian sense of right and justice." His comments suggest that he has combined the spiritual values of his Dakota ancestors with his concept of Christianity.

In his final description of his mature identity, he uses the racial term of "an Indian," rather than a term defining his Indian nation: Dakota or Sioux. Further, his last words, "I am an American," express his allegiance to a national identity that unites Indians and non-Indians.

* * * *

Eastman was the foremost Native American lecturer and author in the early twentieth century. Through his many lectures and books, he not only introduced a wide audience to a Sioux perspective on American Indian cultures, but he also raised the consciousness of his audiences about the injustices suffered by American Indians. Unfortunately, he was unable to achieve his goals of becoming a successful physician within the Indian Service or in private practice. Eastman gained great success, however, as an international symbol of what Native Americans of the twentieth century could become if they combined their tribal concepts of spirituality and reverence for nature with Christianity and Euro-American education.

A. LaVonne Brown Ruoff

Oak Park, Illinois
April 2001

NOTES ON
AMERICAN INDIAN NATIONS

*The tribes described are those of individuals or nations
to which Eastman refers in his autobiographies,* Indian
Boyhood *and* From the Deep Woods to Civilization.

SIOUX

The term Sioux derives from the French version of
the Ojibwa word *nadowe-is-iw,* Little Snakes or
"enemy." The name refers to the conflicts between the
Sioux and the Ojibwa. The earlier name for the combined group was Dakota, meaning "allies." In the
nineteenth and early twentieth centuries, Sioux elders
and scholars sometimes used "Dakota" to refer to the
whole nation. Although some elders continue to use
this term, Sioux people today generally refer to themselves as either Dakota, Nakota, or Lakota. Each group
speaks a different dialect of the Siouan language.

Scholars suggest that the group originated from a
Siouan population that may have occupied the lower
Ohio and middle Mississippi valleys before they dispersed. In the sixteenth and seventeenth centuries,
they moved north and occupied parts of Wisconsin
and most of northern Minnesota. The ancestral
Dakota believe that they always lived in the northern
Great Plains area. If there was a migration, it was outward from the Black Hills.

Originally, the group had seven major divisions,

which were called the *Oceti Sakowin,* or "Seven Council Fires." French missionaries and explorers first contacted them in the mid-seventeenth century. Around this time, conflicts with the Ojibwa and dwindling food supplies caused one group to begin to move south toward the Plains. During the two centuries of their migration, the seven groups became three:

1. *Dakota:* The Santee Dakota consisted of the Mdewakanton (People of Spirit Lake), Wahpeton (Dwellers Among the Leaves), Wahpekute (Shooters Among the Leaves), and Sisseton (People of the Swamp). The Dakota lived in the east and northeast areas of Sioux Territory in the trans-Mississippi region of what is now southern Minnesota. Village dwellers and farmers, the Santee fished, hunted, and gathered wild rice and herbs.

2. *Nakota:* The Yankton group consisted of Ihankton (Campers at the End) and Ihanktonwana (Little Campers at the End). The Assiniboine (Cook with Stones) became associated with the Nakota before reservations were established in the mid-nineteenth century. Living in the southeastern and southern areas of Sioux Territory, the Yankton were semisedentary and served as intermediaries between the farming Santee and the buffalo-hunting Teton. They also quarried pipestone.

3. *Lakota:* The Teton or Western Sioux included seven smaller subdivisions or bands: Sicangu (Burnt Thighs, also called the Brulés), Oohenunpa (Two Kettles), Itazipacola (Without Bows), Miniconjou

(Planters by the Water), the Sihasapa (Black Feet), Hunkpapa (End of the Horn or Entrance), and Oglala (Scatter Their Own). The acknowledged protectors of the Black Hills, the Teton Lakota lived on the Great Plains, west of the Missouri and north of the Arkansas Rivers. Originally the Teton Lakota were hunters, gatherers, and occasional farmers in what is now Minnesota. After they obtained horses in the late seventeenth and early eighteenth centuries, they became buffalo hunters and ranged widely over the Great Plains.

The Sioux now live on reservations in South Dakota, North Dakota, Minnesota, Nebraska, and Montana. Some of the Dakota also live on reserves in Canada.

ARAPAHO

The Arapaho, who speak an Algonquian language, call themselves the *Hinóno' éno,* or the Sky People or Wrong Rooters. Originally, they were joined with the Gros Ventre. They ranged over much of southeastern Wyoming, southwestern Nebraska, eastern Colorado, and the upper northwest area of Kansas.

After they adopted the Plains culture, they split into the Northern and Southern Arapaho. The Northern Arapaho reside on the Wind River Reservation in Wyoming. The land of the Southern Cheyenne–Arapaho Reservation in present-day Oklahoma was allotted to individual tribal members in 1891.

BLACKFEET OR BLACKFOOT

The Algonquian-speaking Blackfeet call themselves the *Nizitapi,* or Real People. In the tribal language, the name for their group is *Amskapi Pikuni.* The Blackfeet nation consisted of the Siksika (Northern Blackfeet), Kainah (Bloods), and Piegans (Poorly Dressed or Torn Robes), who had inhabited the upper Missouri–Saskatchewan River area.

In the nineteenth century, they became known as fierce raiders of the northern Plains. Seven years after federal troops killed many Piegans in January 1870, most of the Blackfeet settled permanently in Canada. The remaining Piegans settled on what became the Blackfeet Reservation in northeastern Montana.

CHEYENNE

Their word for their nation is *Tse-tsehese-staestse,* or People. The term "Cheyenne" is derived from the Lakota word *sha-hi'ye-la,* which means Red Talkers or People of an Alien Speech.

Although the Cheyenne originally inhabited the woodland prairie country of the upper Mississippi valley, some bands later migrated onto the Plains. Between the mid- and late-eighteenth century, they moved into the Black Hills region and became allies with the Arapaho and the Sioux. Several bands of Cheyenne then moved south. The Fort Laramie Treaty of 1851, in which they kept lands between the North Platte and Arkansas Rivers, made permanent the division between the Northern and Southern

Cheyenne. Although they fought against American incursions into their territory, they suffered several devastating defeats. In 1875, the Southern Cheyenne surrendered, as did the Northern Cheyenne in 1879.

Although the Northern Cheyenne were forcibly removed to the Southern Cheyenne–Arapaho Agency in Indian Territory, which is now Oklahoma, they subsequently escaped. Then, in 1884, the government established the Tongue River Reservation for the Northern Cheyenne in southeastern Montana. The Southern Cheyenne–Arapaho Reservation was dissolved by allotment in 1891.

CREE

The original Eastern Woodlands or James Bay Cree of Quebec spread westward, branching off into three additional groups: Western Woodlands or Swampy Cree, Parklands or Woods Cree, and Plains Cree. They speak an Algonquian language. The Cree now live in six Canadian provinces and the Northwest Territories, on Montana's Rocky Boy reservation, and in other locations in the United States.

CROW

The Crow or Absaroke speak a Siouan language. Descended from the Hidtasas of present-day North Dakota, the Crow inhabited the region of the Yellowstone and Bighorn River valleys of what is now eastern Montana and Wyoming. In the 1868 Fort Laramie Treaty, they ceded land to secure alliance with the

whites against their Sioux, Cheyenne, and Blackfeet
enemies. In the 1870s, Crow warriors acted as scouts
for the U.S. Army in its campaigns against the Sioux.
The Crow now live on a reservation in southeastern
Montana.

Fox and Sac or Sauk

In the seventeenth century, the Fox lived in the Green
Bay region of Lake Superior in present-day Wisconsin.
In 1730, they allied themselves with their neighbors,
the Sac, and migrated south near the confluence of the
Rock and Mississippi Rivers. The combined group is
now known as the Mesquakie, "Red Earth People."
Both groups speak an Algonquian language.

Between 1831 and 1842, the government forced the
Mesquakie to cede their lands and move to a reservation in Kansas. In 1869, the government removed them
to Indian Territory (Oklahoma), where one group still
resides. Another group of Mesquakie moved back to
Iowa and bought land in Tama County, where they
continue to live.

Gros Ventre

This Algonquian-speaking nation was also known as
the Waterfall Indians, Big Bellies, and Atsinas. They
call themselves *A'ani'*, or White Clay People.

According to their oral traditions, the Gros Ventre
and Arapaho were once joined and living on the
Canadian Plains. They separated at the Red River in
1700. In the early nineteenth century, they joined

forces with the Blackfeet to fight off the Crow. Most now live at the Fort Belknap Reservation in Montana.

Iowa

Speaking a Siouan language, the Iowa were one of the Border Indians nations that lived on the edge of the Great Plains. They were removed to Indian Territory.

Ojibwa

The Anishinabe are known variously as the Ojibwa, Ojibwe (the official spelling in Minnesota, Wisconsin, and Michigan), Ojibway, and Chippewa. They speak an Algonquian language.

Originally there were three fires or groups: Ojibwa, Ottawa, and Potawatomi. According to their migration myth, they stopped at the Straits of Mackinac, which separates the Upper and Lower Peninsulas of Michigan. There they divided geographically, with the Ojibwa moving north to the St. Marys River.

Now the Ojibwa live in southeastern Ontario, the upper Great Lakes of Canada and the United States, and in North Dakota, Montana, and Saskatchewan.

Otoe

The Otoe or Oto lived along the Nemah and Platte Rivers of eastern Nebraska. They speak a Siouan language. The Otoe and the Missouria were originally two separate tribes. In the late eighteenth century, they allied to fight off the Fox and Sac. By 1882, almost all the Otoe-Missouria had moved to Indian Territory.

OTTAWA

See also Ojibwa. The Ottawa or Odawa, which means Trader or At-Home-Anywhere People, speak an Algonquian language. They trace their origins to Manitoulin Island and to the east and north coasts of Georgian Bay and Bruce Peninsula of Canada.

After contact with Europeans, they moved from Ontario into the Upper and Lower Peninsula of Michigan, Wisconsin, Illinois, Indiana, Ohio, Pennsylvania, Kansas, and Oklahoma. For the past 300 years, they have inhabited the northern Lower Peninsula of Michigan. Although the majority of the Ottawa remained there, the government removed the Roche DeBoeuf and Blachard's Fork bands to Kansas.

In 1867, members of these bands who did not wish to accept individual land allotments moved to Indian Territory (now Oklahoma), where they still live.

PAIUTE

In the period before contact with Europeans, the Paiute ranged from what is now central Oregon in the north to southern California and east to southeastern Wyoming. This group, which speaks a Uto-Aztecan language, includes the Northern Paiute, Southern Paiute, and the Owens Valley Paiute.

Members of the Northern Paiute nation currently live on reservations or in adjacent communities in Nevada, Oregon, and California.

POTAWATOMI

See also Ojibwa. Closely related to the Ottawa and
Ojibwa, the Potawatomi speak an Algonquian lan-
guage and refer to themselves as the *Nishnabek* (The
People).

In the eighteenth century, they occupied the area
from modern-day Milwaukee through Chicago and
northern Indiana, and from the southern part of
Michigan to Detroit.

In the mid-nineteenth century, most were removed
to present-day Kansas and then to Indian Territory,
now Oklahoma. Two bands refused to leave Michigan: the Pokagan band, which lives in southwestern
Michigan, and the Huron band, which lives in south
central Michigan.

SHAWNEE

The Shawnee, who are closely related to the Kick-
apoo, speak an Algonquian language. Their name
derives from *Shawun* (South) or *Shawunogi* (South-
erner). They refer to themselves as *Shawano*.

In the period before contact with Europeans, they
were located on the Ohio River. After the death of
their leader, Tecumseh, in 1813, the bands scattered
and allied with members of other area tribes. The survivors of Tecumseh's defeat, called the Shawnee Nation United Remnant Band, are located in Ohio and
neighboring states.

The federal government removed most of the
Shawnee to Indian Territory, now Oklahoma. There

they divided into three bands: Absentee Shawnee, Eastern Shawnee, and Loyal Shawnee (so called because of their loyalty to the Union during the Civil War).

From the Deep Woods to Civilization

PART I

Excerpts from
Indian Boyhood

FOREWORD

THE North American Indian was the highest type of pagan and uncivilized man. He possessed not only a superb physique but a remarkable mind. But the Indian no longer exists as a natural and free man. Those remnants that now dwell upon the reservations present only a sort of tableau—a fictitious copy of the past.

The following chapters are the imperfect record of my boyish impressions and experiences up to the age of fifteen years. I have put together these fragmentary recollections of my thrilling wild life expressly for the little son who came too late to behold for himself the drama of savage existence. I dedicate this little book, with love, to Ohiyesa the second, my son.

CHARLES ALEXANDER EASTMAN

(Ohiyesa)

I

Early Hardships

WHAT BOY would not be an Indian for a while when he thinks of the freest life in the world? This life was mine. Every day there was a real hunt. There was real game. Occasionally there was a medicine dance away off in the woods where no one could disturb us, in which the boys impersonated their elders, Brave Bull, Standing Elk, High Hawk, Medicine Bear, and the rest. They painted themselves and imitated their fathers and grandfathers to the minutest detail, and accurately too, because they had seen the real thing all their lives.

We were not only good mimics, but we were close students of nature. We studied the habits of animals just as you study your books. We watched the men of our people and represented them in our play, then learned to emulate them in our lives.

No people have a better use of their five senses than the children of the wilderness. We could smell as well as we could hear and see. We could feel and taste as well as we could see and hear. Nowhere has the memory been more carefully developed than in the wild life, and I can still see wherein I owe much to my early training.

Of course I myself do not remember when I first

saw the day, but my brothers have often recalled the event with much mirth, for it was a custom of the Sioux that when a boy was born, his brother must plunge into the water, or roll in the snow naked if it was winter time; and if he was not big enough to do either of these himself, water was thrown on him. If the newborn had a sister, she must be immersed. The idea was that a warrior had come to camp, and the other children must display some act of hardihood.

I was so unfortunate as to be the youngest of five children who, soon after I was born, were left motherless. I had to bear the humiliating name Hakadah, meaning "the pitiful last," until I should earn a more dignified and appropriate name. I was regarded as little more than a plaything by the rest of the children.

My mother, who was known as the handsomest woman of all the Spirit Lake and Leaf-Dweller Sioux, was dangerously ill, and one of the medicine men who attended her said: "Another medicine man has come into existence, but the mother must die. Therefore let him bear the name Mysterious Medicine." But one of the bystanders hastily interfered, saying that an uncle of the child already bore that name, so, for the time, I was only Hakadah.

My beautiful mother, sometimes called the Demi-Goddess of the Sioux,[1] who tradition says had every feature of a Caucasian descent with the exception of

[1] My beautiful mother, sometimes called the Demi-Goddess of the Sioux: Wakantankawin or Mary Nancy Eastman (1830–58) was the daughter of artist Seth Eastman (1809-75) and Wakinajinwin

her luxuriant black hair and deep black eyes, held me tightly to her bosom upon her deathbed, while she whispered a few words to her mother-in-law. She said: "I give you this boy for your own. I cannot trust my own mother with him; she will neglect him and he will surely die."

The woman to whom these words were spoken was below the average in stature, remarkably active for her age (she was then fully sixty), and possessed of as much goodness as intelligence. My mother's judgment concerning her own mother was well founded, for soon after her death that old lady appeared and declared that Hakadah was too young to live without a mother. She offered to keep me until I died, and then she would put me in my mother's grave. Of course, my other grandmother denounced the suggestion as a very wicked one and refused to give me up.

The babe was done up as usual in a movable cradle made from an oak board 2 ½ feet long and 1 ½ feet wide. On one side of it was nailed with brass-headed tacks the richly embroidered sack, which was open in front and laced up and down with buckskin strings. Over the arms of the infant was a wooden bow, the ends of

(Stands Sacred). Nancy's maternal grandfather was Mahpiya Wicasta (Cloud Man, b. 1780), an early convert to Christianity. Eastman's translation of his mother's name as "Demi-Goddess" reflects the contemporary practice of defining Indian religious words in terms comparable to Western European classical and religious nomenclature. Anthropologist Beatrice Medicine (Dakota) translates Wakantankawin as "Holy Woman" or "Sacred Woman." *Wakan* means "holy" or "sacred."

which were firmly attached to the board, so that if the cradle should fall, the child's head and face would be protected. On this bow were hung curious play-things—strings of artistically carved bones and hoofs of deer, which rattled when the little hands moved them.

In this upright cradle I lived, played, and slept the greater part of the time during the first few months of my life. Whether I was made to lean against a lodge pole or was suspended from a bough of a tree while my grandmother cut wood, or whether I was carried on her back or conveniently balanced by another child in a similar cradle hung on the opposite side of a pony, I was still in my oaken bed.

This grandmother, who had already lived through sixty years of hardships, was a wonder to the young maidens of the tribe. She showed no less enthusiasm over Hakadah than she had done when she held her firstborn, the boy's father, in her arms. Every little attention that is due to a loved child she performed with such skill and devotion. She made all my scanty garments and my tiny moccasins with a great deal of taste. It was said by all that I could not have had more attention had my mother been living.

The Dakota women were wont to cut and bring their fuel from the woods and, in fact, to perform most of the drudgery of the camp. This of necessity fell to their lot, because the men must follow the game during the day. Very often my grandmother carried me with her on these excursions; and while she worked, it was her habit to suspend me from a wild grape vine or a spring bough, so that the least breeze would swing the cradle to and fro.

My food was, at first, a troublesome question for my kind foster mother. She cooked some wild rice and strained it, and mixed it with broth made from choice venison. She also pounded dried venison almost to a flour and kept it in water till the nourishing juices were extracted, then mixed with it some pounded maize, which was browned before pounding. This soup of wild rice, pounded venison, and maize was my main-stay. But soon my teeth came—much earlier than the white children usually cut theirs; and then my good nurse gave me a little more varied food, and I did all my own grinding.

Indian children were trained so that they hardly ever cried much in the night. This was very expedient and necessary in their exposed life. In my infancy it was my grandmother's custom to put me to sleep, as she said, with the birds, and to waken me with them, until it became a habit. She did this with an object in view. An Indian must always rise early. In the first place, as a hunter, he finds his game best at daybreak. Secondly, other tribes, when on the warpath, usually make their attack very early in the morning. Even when our people are moving about leisurely, we like to rise before daybreak in order to travel when the air is cool and we are unobserved, perchance, by enemies.

As a little child, it was instilled into me to be silent and reticent. This was one of the most important traits to form in the character of the Indian. As a hunter and warrior, it was considered absolutely necessary to him and was thought to lay the foundations of patience and self-control. There are times when boisterous mirth is indulged in by our people, but the rule is gravity and decorum.

After all, my babyhood was full of interest and the beginnings of life's realities. The spirit of daring was already whispered into my ears. The value of the eagle feather as worn by the warrior had caught my eye. One day, when I was left alone, at scarcely two years of age, I took my uncle's war bonnet and plucked out all its eagle feathers to decorate my dog and myself. So soon the life that was about me had made its impress, and already I desired intensely to comply with all of its demands.

I was a little over four years old at the time of the "Sioux massacre" in Minnesota.[2] In the general turmoil, we took flight into British Columbia,[3] and the

[2]Sioux massacre in Minnesota: Little Crow (Taoyateduta; ca. 1810-63) was chief of the Kaposia band of Mdewakanton. On 18 August 1862, he and a large group of Mdewakanton and Wahpekute warriors of the Santee Dakota Sioux attacked the Lower Sioux Agency. The war quickly spread through southern Minnesota. By 23 September, Gen. Henry H. Sibley (1811-91), a Minnesota politician and soldier, and his men defeated the Santee at the Battle of Wood Lake. During the uprising, 400 to 800 settlers and soldiers were killed.

[3]Late in November or early in December 1862, the first bands of Santee Sioux arrived in the Red River Settlement of Canada. Some moved back and forth between the United States and Canada, pursued by United States forces. Most of the Santees settled in Manitoba, while others moved to Saskatchewan. By 1871,

Medicine Bear, chief of the Upper Yankton Sioux during Eastman's childhood, stereograph, ca. 1860

Courtesy Minnesota Historical Society

Indians who fled to Canada after the 1862 Uprising

Courtesy, Minnesota Historical Society

journey is still vividly remembered by all our family. A yoke of oxen and a lumber wagon were taken from some white farmer and brought home for our conveyance.

How delighted I was when I learned that we were to ride behind those wise-looking animals and in that gorgeously painted wagon! It seemed almost like a living creature to me, this new vehicle with four legs, and the more so when we ran out of axle-grease and the wheels went along squealing like pigs!

The boys found a great deal of innocent fun in jumping from the high wagon while the oxen were leisurely moving along. My elder brothers soon became experts. At last, I mustered up courage enough to join them in this sport. I was sure they stepped on the wheel, so I cautiously placed my moccasined foot upon it. Alas! before I could realize what had happened, I was under the wheels, and had it not been for the neighbor immediately behind us, I might have been run over by the next team as well.

This was my first experience with a civilized vehicle. I cried out all possible reproaches on the white man's team and concluded that a dog-travois (a pair of shafts fastened on either side of the animal and trailing on the ground behind) was good enough for me. I rejoiced that we were moving away from the people who made the wagon that had almost ended my life,

---

there were some eight Canadian Dakota reserves in Manitoba and Saskatchewan. Although Dakotas may have traveled into British Columbia, I find no evidence that they settled there.

and it did not occur to me that I alone was to blame. I could not be persuaded to ride in that wagon again and was glad when we finally left it beside the Missouri River.

The summer after the Minnesota massacre, General Sibley pursued our people across this river. Now the Missouri is considered one of the most treacherous rivers in the world. Even a good modern boat is not safe upon its uncertain current. We were forced to cross in buffalo-skin boats—as round as tubs!

The *Washechu* (white men) were coming in great numbers with their big guns, and while most of our men were fighting them to gain time, the women and the old men made and equipped the temporary boats, braced with ribs of willow. Some of these were towed by two or three women or men swimming in the water, and some by ponies. It was not an easy matter to keep them right side up, with their helpless freight of little children and such goods as we possessed.

In our flight, we little folks were strapped in the saddles or held in front of an older person, and in the long night marches to get away from the soldiers, we suffered from loss of sleep and insufficient food. Our meals were eaten hastily, and sometimes in the saddle. Water was not always to be found. The people carried it with them in bags formed of tripe or the dried pericardium of animals.

Now we were compelled to trespass upon the country of hostile tribes and were harassed by them almost daily and nightly. Only the strictest vigilance saved us.

One day we met with another enemy near the British lines. It was a prairie fire. We were surrounded. Another fire was quickly made, which saved our lives.[4]

One of the most thrilling experiences of the following winter was a blizzard, which overtook us in our wanderings. Here and there, a family lay down in the snow, selecting a place where it was not likely to drift much. For a day and a night we lay under the snow. Uncle struck a long pole beside us to tell us when the storm was over. We had plenty of buffalo robes and the snow kept us warm, but we found it heavy. After a time, it became packed and hollowed out around our bodies, so that we were as comfortable as one can be under the circumstances.

The next day the storm ceased, and we discovered a large herd of buffalo almost upon us. We dug our way out, shot some of the buffaloes, made a fire, and enjoyed a good dinner.

I was now an exile as well as motherless, yet I was not unhappy. Our wanderings from place to place afforded us many pleasant experiences and quite as many hardships and misfortunes. There were times of plenty and times of scarcity, and we had several narrow escapes from death. In savage life, the early spring is the most trying time, and almost all the famines occurred at this period of the year.

The Indians are a patient and a clannish people;

---

[4]Eastman probably refers to the practice of setting a backfire ahead of the main fire. The backfire burns toward the main one, depriving it of fuel so that the two flame out when they meet.

their love for one another is stronger than that of any civilized people I know. If this were not so, I believe there would have been tribes of cannibals among them. White people have been known to kill and eat their companions in preference to starving; but Indians—never!

In times of famine, the adults often denied themselves in order to make food last as long as possible for the children, who were not able to bear hunger as well as the old. As a people, they can live without food much longer than any other nation.

I once passed through one of these hard springs when we had nothing to eat for several days. I well remember six small birds, which constituted breakfast for six families one morning; and then we had no dinner or supper to follow! Soon after this, we came into a region where buffaloes were plenty, and hunger and scarcity were forgotten.

The raids made upon our people by other tribes were frequent, and we had to be constantly on the watch. I remember at one time a night attack was made upon our camp and all our ponies stampeded. Only a few of them were recovered, and our journeys after this misfortune were effected mostly by means of the dog-travois.

The second winter after the massacre, my father[5] and my two older brothers, with several others, were betrayed by a half-breed at Winnipeg to the United

[5]My father: Eastman's father was Many Lightnings, who took as his Christian name Jacob Eastman, adopting his wife's last name.

States authorities. As I was then living with my uncle in another part of the country, I became separated from them for ten years. During all this time we believed that they had been killed by the whites, and I was taught that I must avenge their deaths as soon as I was able to go upon the warpath.

It is wonderful that any children grew up through all the exposures and hardships that we suffered in those days! The frail tepee pitched anywhere, in the winter as well as in the summer, was all the protection that we had against cold and storms. I can recall times when we were snowed in and it was very difficult to get fuel. We were once three days without much fire, and all of this time it stormed violently. There seemed to be no special anxiety on the part of our people; they rather looked upon all this as a matter of course, that the storm would cease when the time came.

I could once endure as much cold and hunger as any of them; but now if I miss one meal or accidentally wet my feet, I feel it as much as if I had never lived in the manner I have described, when it was a matter of course to get myself soaking wet many a time. Even if there was plenty to eat, it was thought better for us to practice fasting sometimes; and hard exercise was kept up continually, both for the sake of health and to prepare the body for the extraordinary exertions that it might, at any moment, be required to undergo. In my own remembrance, my uncle often used to bring home a deer on his shoulder. The distance was sometimes considerable, yet he did not consider it a feat.

The usual custom with us was to eat only two meals a day, and these were served at each end of the day. This rule was not invariable, however, for if there should be any callers, it was Indian etiquette to offer either tobacco or food, or both. The rule of two meals a day was more closely observed by the men—especially the younger men—than by the women and children. This was when the Indians recognized that a true manhood, one of physical activity and endurance, depends upon dieting and regular exercise. No such system is practiced by the reservation Indians of today.

II

My Indian Grandmother

A s a motherless child, I always regarded my good grandmother as the wisest of guides and the best of protectors. It was not long before I began to realize her superiority to most of her contemporaries. This idea was not gained entirely from my own observation, but also from a knowledge of the high regard in which she was held by other women. Aside from her native talent and ingenuity, she was endowed with a truly wonderful memory. No other midwife in her day and tribe could compete with her skill and judgment. Her observations in practice were all preserved in her mind for reference, as systematically as if they had been written upon the pages of a notebook.

I distinctly recall one occasion when she took me with her into the woods in search of medicinal roots.

"Why do you not use all kinds of roots for medicines?" said I.

"Because," she replied, in her quick, characteristic manner, "the Great Mystery does not will us to find things too easily. In that case everybody would be a medicine-giver, and you must learn that there are many secrets the Great Mystery will disclose only to the most worthy. Only those who seek him in fasting and in solitude will receive his signs."

With this and with many similar explanations she wrought in my soul wonderful and lively conceptions of the Great Mystery and of the effects of prayer and solitude.

Our native women gathered all the wild rice, roots, berries, and fruits that formed an important part of our food. This was distinctively a woman's work. Uncheedah (grandmother) understood these matters perfectly, and it became a kind of instinct with her to know just where to look for each edible variety and at what season of the year. This sort of labor gave the Indian women every opportunity to observe and then to study nature after their own fashion; and in this Uncheedah was more acute than most of the men. The abilities of her boys were not all inherited from their father; indeed, the stronger family traits came obviously from her. She was a leader among the native women, and they came to her, not only for medical aid, but for advice in all their affairs.

In bravery she equaled any of the men. This trait, together with her ingenuity and alertness of mind, more than once saved her and her people from destruction. Once, when we were roaming over a region occupied by other tribes, and on a day when most of the men were out upon the hunt, a party of hostile Indians suddenly appeared. Although there were a few men left at home, they were taken by surprise at first and scarcely knew what to do, when this woman came forward and advanced alone to meet our foes. She had gone some distance when some of the men followed her. She met the strangers and offered her hand to them. They accepted her friendly greeting; and as a result of her brave act, we were left unmolested and at peace.

Another story of her was related to me by my father. My grandfather, who was a noted hunter, often wandered away from his band in search of game. In this instance he had with him only his own family of three boys and his wife. One evening, when he returned from the chase, he found to his surprise that she had built a stockade around her tepee.

She had discovered the danger sign in a single footprint, which she saw at a glance was not that of her husband, and she was also convinced that it was not the footprint of a Sioux, from the shape of the moccasin. This ability to recognize footprints is general among the Indians but more marked in certain individuals.

This courageous woman had driven away a party of five Ojibway warriors. They approached the lodge cautiously, but her dog gave timely warning, and she poured into them from behind her defenses the contents of a double-barreled gun, with such good effect that the astonished braves thought it wise to retreat.

I was not more than five or six years old when the Indian soldiers came one day and destroyed our large buffalo-skin tepee. It was charged that my uncle had hunted alone a large herd of buffalo. This was not exactly true. He had unfortunately frightened a large herd while shooting a deer at the edge of the woods.

However, it was customary to punish such an act severely, even though the offense was accidental.

When we were attacked by the police, I was playing in the tepee, and the only other person at home was Uncheedah. I had not noticed their approach, and when the war cry was given by thirty or forty Indians with strong lungs, I thought my little world was coming to an end. Instantly, innumerable knives and tomahawks penetrated our frail home, while bullets went through the poles and tent-fastenings up above our heads.

I hardly know what I did, but I imagine it was just what any other little fellow would have done under like circumstances. My first clear realization of the situation was when Uncheedah had a dispute with the leader, claiming that the matter had not been properly investigated and that none of the policemen had attained to a reputation in war that would justify them in touching her son's own tepee. But alas! our poor dwelling was already an unrecognizable ruin; even the poles were broken into splinters.

The Indian women, after reaching middle age, are usually heavy and lack agility, but my grandmother was in this also an exception. She was fully sixty when I was born; and when I was seven years old, she swam across a swift and wide stream, carrying me on her back because she did not wish to expose me to accident in one of the clumsy round boats of bull-hide that were rigged up to cross the rivers that impeded our way, especially in the springtime. Her strength

and endurance were remarkable. Even after she had
attained the age of eighty-two, she one day walked
twenty-five miles without appearing much fatigued.

I marvel now at the purity and elevated sentiment
possessed by this woman, when I consider the customs and habits of her people at the time. When her
husband died, she was still comparatively a young
woman—still active, clever, and industrious. She was
descended from a haughty chieftain of the Dwellers
Among the Leaves. Although women of her age and
position were held to be eligible to remarriage, and
she had several persistent suitors who were men of
her own age and chiefs, yet she preferred to cherish in
solitude the memory of her husband.

I was very small when my uncle brought home two
Ojibway young women. In the fight in which they
were captured, none of the Sioux war party had been
killed; therefore, they were treated tenderly by the
Sioux women. They were apparently happy, although
of course they felt deeply the losses sustained at the
time of their capture, yet they did not fail to show their
appreciation of the kindnesses received.

As I recall now the remarks made by one of them at
the time of their final release, they appeared to me
quite remarkable. They lived in my grandmother's
family for two years and were then returned to their
people at a great peace council of the two nations.
When they were about to leave my grandmother, the
elder of the two sisters first embraced her and then
spoke somewhat as follows: "You are a brave woman

and a true mother. I understand now why your son so bravely conquered our band and took my sister and myself captive. I hated him at first, but now I admire him, because he did just what my father, my brother, or my husband would have done had they the opportunity. He did even more. He saved us from the tomahawks of his fellow-warriors and brought us to his home to know a noble and brave woman.

"I shall never forget your many favors shown to us. But I must go. I belong to my tribe and I shall return to them. I will endeavor to be a true woman also, and to teach my boys to be generous warriors."

Her sister chose to remain among the Sioux all her life, and she married one of our younger men.

"I shall make the Sioux and the Ojibways," she said, "to be as brothers."

There are many other instances of intermarriage with captive women. The mother of the well-known Sioux chieftain, Wabashaw,[1] was an Ojibway woman. I once knew a woman who was said to be a white captive. She was married to a noted warrior and had a fine family of five boys. She was well accustomed to the Indian ways, and as a child I should not have suspected that she was white. The skins of these people became so sunburned and full of paint that it required a keen eye to distinguish them from the real Indians.

[1] A Mdewakanton Santee chief, Wabashaw died in 1835.

III

An Indian Sugar Camp

WITH THE first March thaw, the thoughts of the
Indian women of my childhood days turned
promptly to the annual sugar making, an industry engaged in chiefly by the old men and women and children. The rest of the tribe went out upon the spring
fur hunt at this season, leaving us at home to make the
sugar.

The first and most important of the necessary uten-
sils were the huge iron and brass kettles for boiling.
Everything else could be made, but these must be
bought, begged, or borrowed. A maple tree was felled
and a log canoe hollowed out, into which the sap was
to be gathered. Little troughs of basswood and
birchen basins were also made to receive the sweet
drops as they trickled from the tree.

As soon as these labors were accomplished, we all
proceeded to the bark sugar house, which stood in
the midst of a fine grove of maples on the bank of the
Minnesota River. We found this hut partially filled
with the snows of winter and the withered leaves of
the preceding autumn, and it must be cleared for use.
In the meantime a tent was pitched outside for a few
days' occupancy. The snow was still deep in the
woods, with a solid crust upon which we could easily

walk; for we usually moved to the sugar house before the sap had actually started, the better to complete our preparations.

My grandmother worked like a beaver in these days (or rather like a muskrat, as the Indians say; for this industrious little animal sometimes collects as many as six or eight bushels of edible roots for the winter, only to be robbed of his store by some of our people). If there was prospect of a good sugaring season, she now made a second and even third canoe to contain the sap. These canoes were afterward utilized by the hunters for their proper purpose.

My grandmother did not confine herself to canoe making. She also collected a good supply of fuel for the fires, for she would not have much time to gather wood when the sap began to flow. Presently the weather moderated and the snow began to melt. The month of April brought showers, which carried most of it off into the Minnesota River. Now the women began to test the trees—moving leisurely among them, axe in hand, and striking a single quick blow to see if the sap would appear. The trees, like people, have their individual characters; some were ready to yield up their lifeblood, while others were more reluctant. Now one of the birchen basins was set under each tree and a hardwood chip driven deep into the cut the axe had made. From the corners of this chip—at first drop by drop, then more freely—the sap trickled into the little dishes.

It is usual to make sugar from maples, but other

trees were also tapped by the Indians. From the birch and ash was made a dark-colored sugar, with a somewhat bitter taste, which was used for medicinal purposes. The box elder yielded a beautiful white sugar, whose only fault was that there was never enough of it!

A log fire was now made in the sugar house, and a row of brass kettles suspended over the blaze. The sap was collected by the women in tin or birchen buckets and poured into the canoes, from which the kettles were kept filled. The hearts of the boys beat high with pleasant anticipation when they heard the welcome hissing sound of the boiling sap! Each boy claimed one kettle for his especial charge. It was his duty to see that the fire was kept up under it, to watch lest it boil over, and finally, when the sap became syrup, to test it upon the snow, dipping it out with a wooden paddle. So frequent were these tests that for the first day or two we consumed nearly all that could be made; and it was not until the sweetness began to pall that my grandmother set herself in earnest to store up sugar for future use. She made it into cakes of various forms, in birchen molds, and sometimes in hollow canes or reeds, and the bills of ducks and geese. Some of it was pulverized and packed in rawhide cases. Being a prudent woman, she did not give it to us after the first month or so, except upon special occasions, and it was thus made to last almost the year around. The smaller candies were reserved as an occasional treat for the little fellows, and the sugar was eaten at feasts with wild rice or parched corn, and also

with pounded dried meat. Coffee and tea were all unknown to us in those days.

I remember on the occasion of our last sugar bush
in Minnesota, that I stood one day outside of our hut
and watched the approach of a visitor—a bent old
man, his hair almost white, and carrying on his back
a large bundle of red willow, or kinnikinick, which the
Indians use for smoking. He threw down his load at
the door and thus saluted us: "You have indeed perfect weather for sugar making."

It was my great-grandfather, Cloud Man, whose
original village was on the shores of Lakes Calhoun
and Harriet, now in the suburbs of the city of Minneapolis. He was the first Sioux chief to welcome the
Protestant missionaries among his people, and a well-
known character in those pioneer days. He brought us
word that some of the peaceful sugar makers near us
on the river had been attacked and murdered by roving Ojibways. This news disturbed us not a little, for
we realized that we too might become the victims of an
Ojibway war party. Therefore we all felt some uneasiness from this time until we returned heavy laden to
our village.

IV

A Midsummer Feast

IT WAS midsummer. Everything that the Santee Sioux had undertaken during the year had been unusually successful. The spring fur hunters had been fortunate, and the heavy winter had proved productive of much maple sugar. The women's patches of maize and potatoes were already sufficiently advanced to use. The Wahpetonwan band of Sioux, the Dwellers Among the Leaves, were awakened to the fact that it was time for the midsummer festivities.

The invitations were bundles of tobacco, and acceptances were sent back from the various bands— the Light Lodges, Dwellers Back from the River, and many others, in similar fashion. Blue Earth, chief of the Dwellers Among the Leaves, was the host.

There were to be many different kinds of athletic games. But the one all-important event of the occasion was the lacrosse game,[1] for which it had been customary to select those two bands that could boast the greater number of fast runners.

[1]lacrosse: American Indians played this stick-ball game before Europeans arrived on the continent. The early French settlers used "lacrosse" to refer to any game played with a curved stick (crosse) and a ball. Players use a netted racket to pick up, hurl, or catch the ball and throw it into or beyond the goal to score a point. A player's hands must not touch the ball. Although non-Indians

31

A meeting was held to appoint some "medicine man" to make the balls that were to be used in the lacrosse contest; and presently the herald announced that this honor now had been conferred upon old Chankpee-yuhah, or Keeps the Club, while every other man of his profession was disappointed. He was a powerful man physically, who had apparently won the confidence of the people by his fine personal appearance and by working upon superstitious minds.

Toward evening he appeared in the circle, leading by the hand a boy about four years old. Closely the little fellow observed every motion of the man; nothing escaped his vigilant black eyes, which seemed constantly to grow brighter and larger, while his exuberant glossy black hair was plaited and wound around his head like that of a Celestial.[2] He wore a bit of swan's down in each ear, which formed a striking contrast with the child's complexion. Further than this, the boy was painted according to the fashion of the age. He held in his hands a miniature bow and arrows.

The medicine man drew himself up in an admirable attitude and proceeded to make his short speech:

"Wahpetonwans, you boast that you run down the elk; you can outrun the Ojibways. Before you all, I dedicate to you this red ball. Kaposias, you claim that no one has a lighter foot than you; you declare that

did not take up the game until sometime in the mid-nineteenth century, lacrosse today is one of the fastest-growing sports.

[2]This was a term formerly used to refer to Chinese immigrants.

you can endure running a whole day without water. To you I dedicate this black ball. Either you or the Leaf-Dwellers will have to drop your eyes and bow your head when the game is over. I wish to announce that if the Wahpetonwans should win, this little warrior shall bear the name Ohiyesa (Winner) through life; but if the Light Lodges should win, let the name be given to any child appointed by them."

The ground selected for the great final game was on a narrow strip of land between a lake and the river. It was about three-quarters of a mile long and a quarter of a mile in width. The spectators had already ranged themselves all along the two sides, as well as at the two ends, which were somewhat higher than the middle. The soldiers appointed to keep order furnished much of the entertainment of the day. They painted artistically and tastefully, according to the Indian fashion, not only their bodies but also their ponies and clubs. They were so strict in enforcing the laws that no one could venture with safety within a few feet of the limits of the field.

Now all of the minor events and feasts, occupying several days' time, had been observed. Heralds on ponies' backs announced that all who intended to participate in the final game were requested to repair to the ground; also that if anyone bore a grudge against another, he was implored to forget his ill feeling until the contest should be over.

The most powerful men were stationed at the halfway ground, while the fast runners were assigned to the back. It was an impressive spectacle—a fine collection of agile forms, almost stripped of garments and painted in wild imitation of the rainbow and sunset sky on human canvas. Some had undertaken to depict the Milky Way across their tawny bodies, and one or two made a bold attempt to reproduce the lightning. Others contented themselves with painting the figure of some fleet animal or swift bird on their muscular chests.

The coiffure of the Sioux lacrosse player has often been unconsciously imitated by the fashionable hairdressers of modern times. Some banged and singed their hair; others did a little more by adding powder. The Grecian knot was located on the wrong side of the head, being tied tightly over the forehead. A great many simply brushed back their long locks and tied them with a strip of otter skin.

For a time, a hundred lacrosse sticks vied with each other, and the wriggling human flesh and paint were all one could see through the cloud of dust. Suddenly there shot swiftly through the air toward the south, toward the Kaposias' goal, the ball. There was a general cheer from their adherents, which echoed back from the white cliff on the opposite side of the Minnesota. First one side, then the other would gain an advantage, and then it was lost, until the herald proclaimed that it was time to change the ball. No victory was in sight for either side.

After a few minutes' rest, the game was resumed. The red ball was now tossed in the air in the usual

Lacrosse Playing Among the Sioux Indians, *Seth Eastman, oil on canvas, 1851*

Courtesy Corcoran Gallery of Art, Washington, D.C., Gift of William Wilson Corcoran

35

Indians Traveling, *Seth Eastman, watercolor, 1850*

way. No sooner had it descended than one of the rushers caught it and away it went northward; again it was fortunate, for it was advanced by one of the same side. The scene was now one of the wildest excitement and confusion. At last, the northward flight of the ball was checked for a moment and a desperate struggle ensued. Cheers and war whoops became general, such as were never equaled in any concourse of savages, and possibly nowhere except at a college football game.

The ball had not been allowed to come to the surface since it reached this point, for there were more than a hundred men who scrambled for it. Suddenly a warrior shot out of the throng like the ball itself! Then some of the players shouted: "Look out for Antelope! Look out for Antelope!" But it was too late. The little sphere had already nestled into Antelope's palm and that fleetest of Wahpetonwans had thrown down his lacrosse stick and set a determined eye upon the northern goal.

Such a speed! He had cleared almost all the opponents' guards—there were but two more. These were the exceptional runners of the Kaposias. As he approached them in his almost irresistible speed, every savage heart thumped louder in the Indian's dusky bosom. In another moment there would be a defeat for the Kaposias or a prolongation of the game. The two men, with a determined look, approached their foe like two panthers prepared to spring; yet he neither slackened his speed nor deviated from his course.

A crash—a mighty shout!—the two Kaposias collided, and the swift Antelope had won the laurels.

The turmoil and commotion at the victors' camp were indescribable. A few beats of a drum were heard, after which the criers hurried along the lines, announcing the last act to be performed at the camp of the Leaf-Dwellers.

The day had been a perfect one. Every event had been a success; and, as a matter of course, the old people were happy, for they largely profited by these occasions. Within the circle formed by the general assembly sat in a group the members of the common council. Blue Earth arose and in a few appropriate and courteous remarks assured his guests that it was not selfishness that led his braves to carry off the honors of the last event, but that this was a friendly contest in which each band must assert its prowess. In memory of this victory, the boy would now receive his name. A loud "Ho-o-o" of approbation reverberated from the edge of the forest.

Half frightened, the little fellow was now brought into the circle, looking very much as if he were about to be executed. Cheer after cheer went up for the awe-stricken boy. Chankpee-yuhah, the medicine man, proceeded to confer the name.

"Ohiyesa (or Winner) shall be thy name henceforth. Be brave, be patient, and thou shalt always win! Thy name is Ohiyesa."

V

An Indian Boy's Training

IT IS commonly supposed that there is no systematic education of their children among the aborigines of this country. Nothing could be further from the truth. All the customs of this primitive people were held to be divinely instituted, and those in connection with the training of children were scrupulously adhered to and transmitted from one generation to another.

Very early, the Indian boy assumed the task of preserving and transmitting the legends of his ancestors and his race. Almost every evening a myth, or a true story of some deed done in the past, was narrated by one of the parents or grandparents, while the boy listened with parted lips and glistening eyes. On the following evening, he was usually required to repeat it. If he was not an apt scholar, he struggled long with his task; but as a rule, the Indian boy is a good listener and has a good memory, so that the stories were tolerably well mastered. The household became his audience, by which he was alternately criticized and applauded.

This sort of teaching at once enlightens the boy's mind and stimulates his ambition. His conception of his own future career becomes a vivid and irresistible force. Whatever there is for him to learn must be learned; whatever qualifications are necessary to be a truly great man he must seek at any expense of danger and hardship. Such was the feeling of the imaginative and brave young Indian. It became apparent to him in early life that he must accustom himself to rove alone and not to fear or dislike the impression of solitude.

It seems to be a popular idea that all the characteristic skill of the Indian is instinctive and hereditary. This is a mistake. All the stoicism and patience of the Indian are acquired traits, and continual practice alone makes him master of the art of woodcraft. Physical training and dieting were not neglected. I remember that I was not allowed to have beef soup or any warm drink. The soup was for the old men. General rules for the young were never to take their food very hot, nor to drink much water.

My uncle, who educated me up to the age of fifteen years, was a strict disciplinarian and a good teacher.

All boys were expected to endure hardship without complaint. In savage warfare, a young man must, of course, be an athlete and used to undergoing all sorts of privations. He must be able to go without food and water for two or three days without displaying any weakness, or to run for a day and a night without any rest. He must be able to traverse a pathless and wild country without losing his way either in the daytime or nighttime. He cannot refuse to do any of these things if he aspires to be a warrior.

Sometimes my uncle would waken me very early in the morning and challenge me to fast with him all day. I had to accept the challenge. We blackened our faces with charcoal so that every boy in the village would know that I was fasting for the day. Then the little tempters would make my life a misery until the merciful sun hid behind the western hills.

I can scarcely recall the time when my own stern teacher began to give sudden war whoops over my head in the morning while I was sound asleep. He expected me to leap up with perfect presence of mind, always ready to grasp a weapon of some sort and to give a shrill whoop in reply. If I was sleepy or startled and hardly knew what I was about, he would ridicule me and say that I need never expect to sell my scalp dear. Often he would vary these tactics by shooting off his gun just outside of the lodge while I was yet asleep, at the same time giving bloodcurdling yells. After a time I became used to this.

When Indians went upon the warpath, it was their custom to try the new warriors thoroughly before coming to an engagement. For instance, when they were near a hostile camp, they would select novices to go after the water and make them do all sorts of things to prove their courage. In accordance with this idea, my uncle used to send me off after water when we camped after dark in a strange place. Perhaps the country was full of wild beasts, and, for aught I knew, there might be scouts from hostile bands of Indians lurking in that very neighborhood.

With all this, our manners and morals were not neglected. I was made to respect the adults and especially the aged. I was not allowed to join in their discussions, nor even to speak in their presence, unless requested to do so. Indian etiquette was very strict, and among the requirements was that of avoiding the direct address. A term of relationship or some title of courtesy was commonly used instead of the personal name by those who wished to show respect. We were taught generosity to the poor and reverence for the Great Mystery. Religion was the basis of all Indian training.

In the old days, no young man was allowed to use tobacco in any form until he had become an acknowledged warrior and had achieved a record. If a youth should seek a wife before he had reached the age of twenty-two or twenty-three and been recognized as a brave man, he was sneered at and considered an ill-bred Indian. He must also be a skillful hunter. An Indian cannot be a good husband unless he brings home plenty of game.

These precepts were in the line of our training for the wild life because the Indian boy was a prince of the wilderness. He had but a very little work to do during the period of his boyhood. His principal occupation was the practice of a few simple arts in warfare and the chase. Aside from this, he was master of his time.

Whatever was required of us boys was quickly performed; then the field was clear for our games and play. There was always a keen competition among us. We felt very much as our fathers did in hunting and war—each one strove to excel all the others.

It is true that our savage life was a precarious one,

and full of dreadful catastrophes; however, this never prevented us from enjoying our sports to the fullest extent. As we left our tepees in the morning, we were never sure that our scalps would not dangle from a pole in the afternoon! It was an uncertain life to be sure. Yet we observed that the fawns skipped and played happily while the gray wolves might be peeping forth from behind the hills, ready to tear them limb from limb.

Our sports were molded by the life and the customs of our people; indeed, we practiced only what we expected to do when grown. Our games were feats with the bow and the arrow, foot and pony races, wrestling, swimming, and imitation of the customs and habits of our fathers. We had sham fights with mud balls and willow wands; we played lacrosse, made war upon bees, shot winter arrows (which were used only in that season), and coasted upon the ribs of animals and buffalo robes.

Occasionally, we also played "white man." Our knowledge of the paleface was limited, but we had learned that he brought goods whenever he came and that our people exchanged furs for his merchandise. We also knew that his complexion was pale, that he had short hair on his head and long hair on his face, and that he wore a coat, trousers, and hat, and did not patronize blankets in the daytime. This was the picture we had formed of the white man.

So we painted two or three of our number with white clay and put on them birchen hats we sewed up for the occasion, fastened a piece of fur to their chins for a beard, and altered their costumes as much as lay within our power. The white of the birchbark was made to answer for their white shirts. Their merchandise consisted of sand for sugar, wild beans for coffee, dried leaves for tea, pulverized earth for gunpowder, pebbles for bullets, and clear water for the dangerous "spirit-water." We traded for these goods with skins of squirrels, rabbits, and small birds.

It will be no exaggeration to say that the life of the Indian hunter was a life of fascination. From the moment that he lost sight of his rude home in the midst of the forest, his untutored mind lost itself in the myriad beauties and forces of nature. Yet he never forgot his personal danger from some lurking foe or savage beast, however absorbing was his passion for the chase.

I was scarcely over three years old when I stood one morning just outside our buffalo-skin tepee, with my little bow and arrows in my hand, and gazed up among the trees. Suddenly the instinct to chase and kill seized me powerfully. Just then a bird flew over my head and then another caught my eye, as it balanced itself upon a swaying bough. Everything else was forgotten, and in that moment I had taken my first step as a hunter.

Our hunting varied with the season of the year and the nature of the country which was for the time our home. Our chief weapon was the bow and arrows, and perhaps, if we were lucky, a knife was possessed by someone in the crowd. In the olden times, knives and hatchets were made from bone and sharp stones.

For fire we used a flint with a spongy piece of dry wood and a stone to strike with. Another way of starting fire was for several of the boys to sit down in a circle and rub two pieces of dry, spongy wood together, one after another, until the wood took fire.

We hunted in company a great deal, though it was a common thing for a boy to set out for the woods quite alone, and he usually enjoyed himself fully as much. Our game consisted mainly of small birds, rabbits, squirrels, and grouse. Fishing, too, occupied much of our time. We hardly ever passed a creek or a pond without searching for some signs of fish. When fish were present, we always managed to get some.

It became a necessary part of our education to learn to prepare a meal while out hunting. It is a fact that most Indians will eat the liver and some other portions of large animals raw, but they do not eat fish or birds uncooked. Neither will they eat a frog or an eel. On our boyish hunts, we often went on until we found ourselves a long way from our camp, when we would kindle a fire and roast a part of our game.

Generally we broiled our meat over the coals on a stick. We roasted some of it over the open fire. But the best way to cook fish and birds is in the ashes, under a big fire. We take the fish fresh from the creek or lake, have a good fire on the sand, dig in the sandy ashes, and bury it deep. The same thing is done in case of a bird, only we wet the feathers first. When it is done, the scales or feathers and skin are stripped off whole, and the delicious meat retains all its juices and flavor. We pulled it off as we ate, leaving the bones undisturbed.

Our people had also a method of boiling without pots or kettles. A large piece of tripe was thoroughly washed and the ends tied, then suspended between four stakes driven into the ground and filled with cold water. The meat was then placed in this novel receptacle and boiled by means of the addition of red-hot stones.

VI

Hakadah's First Offering

"HAKADAH, coowah!" was the sonorous call that came from a large tepee in the midst of the Indian encampment. In answer to the summons, there emerged from the woods, only a few steps away, a boy, accompanied by a splendid black dog.

He hastened to the tent from which he had been summoned, carrying in his hands a bow and arrows gorgeously painted, while the small birds and squirrels that he had killed with these weapons dangled from his belt.

Within the tent sat two old women, one on each side of the fire. Uncheedah was the boy's grandmother, who had brought up the motherless child. Wahchewin was only a caller, but she had been invited to remain and assist in the first personal offering of Hakadah to the Great Mystery.

This was a matter that had, for several days, pretty much monopolized Uncheedah's mind. It was her custom to see to this when each of her children attained the age of eight summers.

She believed that her influence had helped to regulate and develop the characters of her sons to the height of savage nobility and strength of manhood.

The boy came rushing into the lodge, followed by

his dog Ohitika, who was wagging his tail, as if to say: "Master and I are really hunters!"

Hakadah breathlessly gave a descriptive narrative of the killing of each bird and squirrel as he pulled them off his belt and threw them before his grandmother.

"Sit down here," said Uncheedah to the boy. "I have something to say to you. You see that you are now almost a man. Observe the game you have brought me! It will not be long before you will leave me, for a warrior must seek opportunities to make him great among his people.

"You must endeavor to equal your father and grandfather," she went on. "They were warriors and feast-makers. But it is not the poor hunter who makes many feasts. Do you not remember the Legend of the Feast-Maker, who gave forty feasts in twelve moons? And have you forgotten the story of the warrior who sought the will of the Great Mystery? Today you will make your first offering to him.

"You must give up one of your belongings— whichever is dearest to you—for this is to be a sacrificial offering."

This somewhat confused the boy; not that he was selfish, but rather uncertain as to what would be the most appropriate thing to give. Then, too, he supposed that his grandmother referred to his ornaments and playthings only. So he volunteered: "I can give up my best bow and arrows, and all the paints I have, and my bear's claws necklace, Grandmother!"

"Are these the thing dearest to you?"

"Not the bow and arrows, but the paints will be very hard to get, for there are no white people near; and the necklace—it is not easy to get one like it again."

"But think, my boy, you have not yet mentioned the thing that will be a pleasant offering to the Great Mystery."

The boy looked into the woman's face with a puzzled expression.

"I have nothing else as good as those things I have named, Grandmother, unless it is my spotted pony; and I am sure that the Great Mystery will not require a little boy to make him so large a gift."

Uncheedah was not satisfied with the boy's free offerings. Perhaps it had not occurred to him what she really wanted. But Uncheedah knew where his affection was vested. His faithful dog, his pet and companion—Hakadah was almost inseparable from the loving beast. She was sure that it would be difficult to obtain his consent to sacrifice the animal, but she ventured upon a final appeal.

"You must remember," she said, "that in this offering you will call upon him who looks at you from every creation. In the wind you hear him whisper to you. He gives his war whoop in the thunder. He watches you by day with his eye, the sun; at night, he gazes upon your sleeping countenance through the moon. In short, it is the Mystery of Mysteries, who controls all things, to whom you make your first offering. By this act, you will ask him to grant to you what he has granted to few men. I know you wish to be a great warrior and hunter. I am not prepared to see my Hakadah show any cowardice, for the love of possessions is a woman's trait and not a brave's."

During the speech, the boy had been completely aroused to the spirit of manliness, and in his excitement was willing to give up anything he had—even his pony! But he was unmindful of his friend and companion, Ohitika, the dog! So scarcely had Uncheedah finished speaking, when he almost shouted:

"Grandmother, I will give up any of my possessions for the offering to the Great Mystery. You may select what you think will be most pleasing to him."

There were two silent spectators of this little dialogue. One was Wahchewin; the other was Ohitika. The woman had been invited to stay, although only a neighbor. The dog, by force of habit, had taken up his usual position by the side of his master when they entered the tepee. Without moving a muscle, save those of his eyes, he had been a close observer.

Had the dog but moved once to attract the attention of his little friend, he might have been dissuaded from that impetuous exclamation: "Grandmother, I will give up any of my possessions!"

It was hard for Uncheedah to tell the boy that he must part with his dog.

"Hakadah," she proceeded cautiously, "you are a young brave. I know, though young, your heart is strong and your courage is great. You will be pleased to give up the dearest thing you have for your first offering. You must give up Ohitika. He is brave; and you, too, are brave. He will not fear death; you will bear his loss bravely. Come—here are four bundles of paints and a filled pipe—let us go to the place."

When the last words were uttered, Hakadah did not seem to hear them. He was simply unable to speak. To a civilized eye, he would have appeared at that moment like a copper statue. His bright black eyes were fast melting in floods of tears, when he caught his grandmother's eye and recollected her oft-repeated adage: "Tears for woman and the war whoop for man to drown the sorrow!"

He swallowed two or three very big mouthfuls of heartache.

"Grandmother, my Brave will have to die! Let me tie together two of the prettiest tails of the squirrels that he and I killed this morning, to show to the Great Mystery what a hunter he has been. Let me paint him myself."

This request Uncheedah could not refuse, and she left the pair alone for a few minutes, while she went to ask Wacoota to execute Ohitika.

Every Indian boy knows that when a warrior is about to meet death, he must sing a death dirge. Hakadah thought of his Ohitika as a person who would meet death without a struggle, so he began to sing a dirge for him, at the same time hugging him tight to himself. As if he were a human being, he whispered in his ear:

"Be brave, my Ohitika! I shall remember you the

first time that I am upon the warpath in the Ojibway country."

At last he heard Uncheedah talking with a man outside the tepee, so he quickly took up his paints. Ohitika was a jet-black dog, with a silver tip on the end of his tail and on his nose, one white paw and a white star upon a protuberance between his ears. Hakadah knew that a man who prepares for death usually paints with red and black. Nature had partially provided Ohitika in this respect, so that only red was required, and this Hakadah supplied generously.

Then he took off a piece of red cloth and tied it around the dog's neck; to this he fastened two of the squirrel tails and a wing from the oriole they had killed that morning.

Just then it occurred to him that good warriors always mourn for their departed friends and the usual mourning was black paint. He loosened his black braided locks, ground a dead coal, mixed it with bear's oil, and rubbed it on his entire face.

During this time every hole in the tent was occupied with an eye. Among the lookers-on was his grandmother. She was very near relenting. Had she not feared the wrath of the Great Mystery, she would have been happy to call out to the boy: "Keep your dear dog, child!"

As it was, Hakadah came out of the tent with his face looking like an eclipsed moon, leading his beautiful dog, who was even handsomer than ever with the red touches on his specks of white.

It was now Uncheedah's turn to struggle with the storm and burden in her soul. But the boy was emboldened by the people's admiration of his bravery and did not shed a tear. As soon as she was able to speak, the loving grandmother said: "No, my young brave, not so! You must not mourn for your first offering. Wash your face and then we will go."

The boy obeyed, submitted Ohitika to Wacoota with a smile, and walked off with his grandmother and Wahchewin. They followed a well-beaten footpath leading along the bank of the Assiniboine River, through a beautiful grove of oak, and finally around and under a very high cliff. The murmuring of the river came up from just below. On the opposite side was a perpendicular white cliff, from which extended back a gradual slope of land, clothed with the majestic mountain oak. The scene was impressive and wild.

Wahchewin had paused without a word when the little party reached the edge of the cliff. It had been arranged between her and Uncheedah that she should wait there for Wacoota, who was to bring as far as that the portion of the offering with which he had been entrusted.

The boy and his grandmother descended the bank, following a tortuous footpath until they reached the water's edge. Then they proceeded to the mouth of an immense cave some fifty feet above the river, under the cliff. A little stream of limpid water trickled down from a spring within the cave. The little watercourse served as a sort of natural staircase for the visitors. A cool, pleasant atmosphere exhaled from the mouth of the cavern. Really it was a shrine of nature, and it is not strange that it was so regarded by the tribe.

A feeling of awe and reverence came to the boy. "It is the home of the Great Mystery," he thought to himself; and the impressiveness of his surroundings made him forget his sorrow.

Very soon Wahchewin came with some difficulty to the steps. She placed the body of Ohitika upon the ground in a lifelike position and again left the two alone.

As soon as she disappeared from view, Uncheedah, with all solemnity and reverence, unfastened the leather strings that held four small bundles of paints and one of tobacco, while a filled pipe was laid beside the dead Ohitika. She scattered paints and tobacco all about. Again they stood for a few moments silently; then she drew a deep breath and began her prayer to the Great Mystery:

"O, Great Mystery, we hear thy voice in the rushing waters below us! We hear thy whisper in the great oaks above! Our spirits are refreshed with thy breath from within this cave. O, hear our prayer. Behold this little boy and bless him! Make him a warrior and hunter as great as thou didst make his father and grandfather."

And with this prayer the little warrior had completed his first offering.

VII

Life in the Woods

THE MONTH of September recalls to every Indian's mind the season of the fall hunt. I remember one such expedition typical of many. Our party appeared on the northwestern side of Turtle Mountain,[1] for we had been hunting buffaloes all summer in the region of the Mouse River, between that mountain and the upper Missouri.

As our cone-shaped tepees rose in clusters along the outskirts of the heavy forest that clothed the sloping side of the mountain, the scene below was gratifying to a savage eye. The rolling yellow plains were checkered with herds of buffaloes. Along the banks of the streams that ran down from the mountains were also many elk, which usually appear at morning and evening, and disappear into the forest during the warmer part of the day. Deer, as well, were plenty, and the brooks were alive with trout. Here and there the streams were dammed by the industrious beaver.

In the interior of the forest, there were lakes with many islands, where moose, elk, deer, and bears were abundant. The waterfowl were wont to gather here in

[1]Turtle Mountain is located north of Bottineau, North Dakota, near the Canadian border. Turtle Mountain Provincial Park is in Manitoba, near the North Dakota border.

great numbers, among them the crane, the swan, the loon, and many of the smaller kinds. The forest also was filled with a great variety of birds. Here the partridge drummed his loudest, the whippoorwill sang with spirit, and the hooting owl reigned in the night.

To me, as a boy, this wilderness was a paradise. It was a land of plenty. To be sure, we did not have any of the luxuries of civilization, but we had every convenience and opportunity and luxury of nature. We had also the gift of enjoying our good fortune, whatever dangers might lurk about us; and the truth is that we lived in blessed ignorance of any life that was better than our own.

As soon as hunting in the woods began, the customs regulating it were established. The council tepee no longer existed. A hunting bonfire was kindled every morning at daybreak, at which each brave must appear and report. The man who failed to do this before the party set out on the day's hunt was harassed by ridicule. As a rule, the hunters started before sunrise, and the brave who was announced throughout the camp as the first one to return with a deer on his back was a man to be envied.

The legendteller, old Smoky Day, was chosen herald of the camp, and it was he who made the announcements. After supper was ended, we heard his powerful voice resound among the tepees in the forest. He would then name a man to kindle the bonfire the next morning. His suit of fringed buckskin set off his splendid physique to advantage.

Scarcely had the men disappeared in the woods each morning than all the boys sallied forth, apparently engrossed in their games and sports, but in reality competing actively with one another in quickness of observation. As the day advanced, they all kept the sharpest possible lookout. Suddenly there would come the shrill "Woo-coo-hoo!" at the top of a boy's voice, announcing the bringing in of a deer. Immediately all the other boys took up the cry, each one bent on getting ahead of the rest. Now we all saw the brave Wacoota fairly bent over by his burden, a large deer that he carried on his shoulders. His fringed buckskin shirt was besprinkled with blood. He threw down the deer at the door of his wife's mother's home, according to custom, and then walked proudly to his own. At the door of his father's tepee he stood for a moment straight as a pine tree, and then entered.

When a bear was brought in, a hundred or more of these urchins were wont to make the woods resound with their voices: "The brave White Rabbit brings a bear! Wah! wah! wah!"

All day these singsong cheers were kept up, as the game was brought in. At last, toward the close of the afternoon, all the hunters had returned, and happiness and contentment reigned absolute, in a fashion I have never observed among the white people, even in the best of circumstances. The men were lounging and smoking; the women actively engaged in the preparation of the evening meal and the care of the meat. The choicest of the game was cooked and then offered to the Great Mystery, with all accompanying ceremonies. This we called the "medicine feast." Even the women, as they lowered the boiling pot, or the fragrant roast of venison ready to serve, would first whisper: "Great Mystery, do thou partake of this venison, and still be gracious!" This was the commonly said "grace."

Everything went smoothly with us on this occasion when we first entered the woods. Nothing was wanting to our old way of living. The killing of deer and elk and moose had to be stopped for a time, since meat was so abundant that we had no use for them any longer. Only the hunting for pelts, such as those of the bear, beaver, marten, and otter were continued. But whenever we lived in blessed abundance, our braves were wont to turn their thoughts to other occupations—especially the hot-blooded youths whose ambition it was to do something noteworthy.

At just such moments as this there are always a number of priests in readiness, whose vocation it is to see into the future, and each of whom consults his particular interpreter of the Great Mystery. (This ceremony is called by the white people "making medicine.") To the priests the youthful braves hint their impatience for the warpath. Soon comes the desired dream of prophecy or vision to favor their departure.

Our young men presently received their sign, and for a few days all was hurry and excitement. On the appointed morning we heard the songs of the warriors and the wailing of the women, by which they

Dakota women and children guarding corn from blackbirds, 1862

Courtesy Minnesota Historical Society

Dakota woman sitting in her tepee, 1865

bade adieu to each other and the eligible braves. Headed by old Hotanka or Loud-Voiced Raven, they set out for Gros Ventre country.

Our older heads, to be sure, had expressed some disapproval of the undertaking, for the country in which we were roaming was not our own, and we were likely at any time to be taken to task by its rightful owners. The plain truth of the matter was that we were intruders. Hence the more thoughtful among us preferred to be at home and to achieve what renown they could get by defending their homes and families. The young men, however, were so eager for action and excitement that they must go off in search of it.

From the early morning when these braves left us, led by the old war priest, Loud-Voiced Raven, the anxious mothers, sisters, and sweethearts counted the days. Old Smoky Day would occasionally get up early in the morning and sing a "strong-heart" song for his absent grandson. I still seem to hear the hoarse, cracked voice of the ancient singer as it resounded among the woods. For a long time our roving community enjoyed unbroken peace, and we were spared any trouble or disturbance. Our hunters often brought in a deer or elk or bear for fresh meat. The beautiful lakes furnished us with fish and wildfowl for variety. Their placid waters, as the autumn advanced, reflected the variegated colors of the changing foliage.

It is my recollection that we were at this time encamped in the vicinity of the Turtle Mountain's Heart. It is to the highest cone-shaped peak that the Indians aptly give this appellation. Our campground for two months was within a short distance of the peak, and the men made it a point to often send one of the number to the top. It was understood between them and the war party that we were to remain near this spot; and on their return trip the latter were to give the smoke sign, which we would answer.

One day, as we were camping on the shore of a large lake with several islands, signs of moose were discovered, and the men went off to them on rafts, carrying their flintlock guns in anticipation of finding two or three of the animals. We little fellows, as usual, were playing down by the sandy shore, when we spied what seemed like the root of a great tree floating toward us. But on a closer scrutiny we discovered our error. It was the head of a huge moose, swimming for his life! Fortunately for him, none of the men remained at home.

According to our habit, we little urchins disappeared in an instant, like young prairie chickens, in the long grass. I was not more than eight years old, yet I tested the strength of my bow string and adjusted my sharpest and best arrow for immediate service. My heart leaped violently as the homely but imposing animal neared the shore. I was undecided for a moment whether I would not leave my hiding place and give a war whoop as soon as he touched the sand. Then I thought I would keep still and let him have my boy weapon; and the only regret that I had was that he would, in all probability, take it with him, and I should be minus one good arrow.

"Still," I thought, "I shall claim to be the smallest boy whose arrow was ever carried away by a moose." That was enough. I gathered myself into a bunch, all ready to spring. As the long-legged beast pulled himself dripping out of the water and shook off the drops from his long hair, I sprang to my feet. I felt some of the water in my face! I gave him my sharpest arrow with all the force I could muster, right among the floating ribs. Then I uttered my war whoop.

The moose did not seem to mind the miniature weapon, but he was very much frightened by our shrill yelling. He took to his long legs and in a minute was out of sight.

The leaves had now begun to fall, and the heavy frosts made the nights very cold. We were forced to realize that the short summer of that region had said adieu! Still we were gay and light-hearted, for we had plenty of provisions, and no misfortune had yet overtaken us in our wanderings over the country for nearly three months.

One day old Smoky Day returned from the daily hunt with an alarm. He had seen a sign—a smoke sign. This had not appeared in the quarter that they were anxiously watching—it came from the east. After a long consultation among the men, it was concluded from the nature and duration of the smoke that it proceeded from an accidental fire. It was further surmised that the fire was not made by Sioux, since it was out of their country, but by a war party of Ojibways, who were accustomed to use matches when lighting their pipes, and to throw them carelessly away. It was thought that a little time had been spent in an attempt to put it out.

The council decreed that a strict lookout should be established in behalf of our party. Every day a scout was appointed to reconnoiter in the directions of the smoke. It was agreed that no gun should be fired for twelve days. All our signals were freshly rehearsed among the men. The women and old men went so far as to dig little convenient holes around their lodges, for defense in case of a sudden attack. And yet an Ojibway scout would not have suspected, from the ordinary appearance of the camp, that the Sioux had become aware of their neighborhood! Scouts were stationed just outside of the village at night. They had been so trained as to rival an owl or cat in their ability to see in the dark.

The twelve days passed by, however, without bringing any evidence of the nearness of the supposed Ojibway war party, and the lookout established for purposes of protection was abandoned. Soon after this, one morning at dawn, we were aroused by the sound of the unwelcome war whoop. Although only a child, I sprang up and was about to rush out, as I had been taught to do; but my good grandmother pulled me down and gave me a sign to lay flat on the ground. I sharpened my ears and lay still.

All was quiet in camp, but at some little distance from us there was a lively encounter. I could distinctly hear the old herald, shouting and yelling in exasperation. "Whoo! whoo!" was the signal of distress, and I could almost hear the pulse of my own blood vessels.

Closer and closer the struggle came, and still the women appeared to grow more and more calm. At last a tremendous charge by the Sioux put the enemy to flight; there was a burst of yelling. Alas! My friend and teacher, old Smoky Day, was silent. He had been pierced to the heart by an arrow from the Ojibways.

Although successful, we had lost two of our men, Smoky Day and White Crane, and this incident, although hardly unexpected, darkened our peaceful sky. The camp was filled with songs of victory, mingled with the wailing of the relatives of the slain. The mothers of the youths who were absent on the warpath could no longer conceal their anxiety.

One frosty morning—for it was then near the end of October—the weird song of a solitary brave was heard. In an instant the camp was thrown into indescribable confusion. The meaning of this was clear as day to everybody—all of our war party were killed, save the one whose mournful song announced the fate of his companions. The lonely warrior was Bald Eagle.

The village was convulsed with grief; for in sorrow, as in joy, every Indian shares with all the others. The old women stood still, wherever they might be, and wailed dismally, at intervals chanting the praises of the departed warriors. The wives went a little way from their tepees and there audibly mourned; but the young maidens wandered farther away from the camp, where no one could witness their grief. The old men joined in the crying and singing. To all appearances the most unmoved of all were the warriors, whose tears must be poured forth in the country of the enemy to embitter their vengeance. These sat silently within their lodges and strove to conceal their feelings behind a stoical countenance, but they would probably have failed had not the soothing weed come to their relief.

The first sad shock over, then came the change of habiliments. In savage usage, the outward expression of mourning surpasses that of civilization. The Indian mourner gives up all his good clothing and contents himself with scanty and miserable garments. Blankets are cut in two, and the hair is cropped short. Often a devoted mother will scarify her arms or legs; a sister or a young wife will cut off all her beautiful hair and disfigure herself by undergoing hardships. Fathers and brothers blacken their faces and wear only the shabbiest garments. Such was the spectacle that our people presented when the bright autumn was gone and the cold shadow of winter and misfortune had fallen upon us. "We must suffer," said they—"the Great Mystery is offended."

VIII

A Winter Camp

WHEN I WAS about twelve years old, we wintered upon the Mouse River, west of Turtle Mountain. It was one of the coldest winters I ever knew, and was so regarded by the old men of the tribe.

The summer before, there had been plenty of buffalo upon that side of the Missouri, and our people had made many packs of dried buffalo meat and cached them in different places so that they could get them in case of need. There were many black-tailed deer and elk along the river, and grizzlies were to be found in the open country. Apparently there was no danger of starvation, so our people thought to winter there; but it proved to be a hard winter.

There was a great snowfall, and the cold was intense. The snow was too deep for hunting, and the main body of buffalo had crossed the Missouri, where it was too far to go after them. There was still fresh meat to be had, but it was not secured without a great deal of difficulty.

No ponies could be used. The men hunted on snowshoes until after the Moon of Sore Eyes (March), when after a heavy thaw a crust was formed on the snow. It was then that our people hunted buffalo with dogs—an unusual expedient.

67

Sleds were made of buffalo ribs and of hickory saplings, the runners bound with rawhide with the hair side down. These slipped smoothly over the icy crust. Only small men rode on the sleds. When buffalo were reported by the hunting scouts, everybody had his dog team ready. All went under orders from the police and approached the herd under cover until they came within charging distance.

The men had their bows and arrows, and a few had guns. The huge animals could not run fast in the deep snow. They all followed a leader, trampling out a narrow path. The dogs with their drivers soon caught up with them on each side, and the hunters brought many of the buffaloes down.

I remember when the party returned, late in the night. The men came in single file, well loaded, and each dog following his master with an equally heavy load. Both men and animal were white with frost.

We boys had waited impatiently for their arrival. As soon as we spied them coming, a buffalo-hunting whistle was started, and every urchin in the village added his voice to the weird sound, while the dogs who had been left at home joined with us in chorus. The men, wearing their buffalo moccasins with the hair inside and robes of the same, came home hungry and exhausted.

It is often supposed that the dog in the Indian camp is a useless member of society, but it is not so in the wild life. We found him one of the most useful of domestic animals, especially in an emergency.

While at this camp, a ludicrous incident occurred that is still told about the campfires of the Sioux. One day the men were hunting on snowshoes and contrived to get within a short distance of the buffalo before they made the attack. It was impossible to run fast, but the huge animals were equally unable to get away. Many were killed. Just as the herd reached an open plain, one of the buffaloes stopped and finally lay down. Three of the men who were pursuing him shortly came up. The animal was severely wounded but not dead.

"I shall crawl up to him from behind and stab him," said Wamedee; "we cannot wait here for him to die." The others agreed. Wamedee was not considered especially brave, but he took out his knife and held it between his teeth. He then approached the buffalo from behind and suddenly jumped astride his back.

The animal was dreadfully frightened and struggled to his feet. Wamedee's knife fell to the ground, but he held on by the long shaggy hair. He had a bad seat, for he was upon the buffalo's hump. There was no chance to jump off; he had to stay on as well as he could.

"Hurry! hurry! shoot! shoot!" he screamed, as the creature plunged and kicked madly in the deep snow. Wamedee's face looked deathly, they said; but his two friends could not help laughing. He was still calling upon them to shoot, but when the others took aim, he would cry: "Don't shoot! don't shoot! you will kill me!" At last the animal fell down with him; but

Wamedee's two friends also fell down exhausted with laughter. He was ridiculed as a coward thereafter.

It was on this very hunt that the chief Mato was killed by a buffalo. It happened in this way. He had wounded the animal but not fatally, so he shot two more arrows at him from a distance. Then the buffalo became desperate and charged upon him. In his flight Mato was tripped by sticking one of his snowshoes into a snowdrift, from which he could not extricate himself in time. The bull gored him to death. The creek upon which this happened is now called Mato Creek.

A little way from our camp there was a log village of French Canadian half-breeds, but the two villages did not intermingle. About the Moon of Difficulty (January) we were initiated into some of the peculiar customs of our neighbors. In the middle of the night, there was a firing of guns throughout their village. Some of the people thought they had been attacked and went over to assist them, but to their surprise they were told that this was the celebration of the birth of the new year!

Our men were treated to *minnewakan* or spirit-water, and they came home crazy and foolish. They talked loud and sang all the rest of the night. Finally our head chief ordered his young men to tie these men up and put them in a lodge by themselves. He gave orders to untie them "when the evil spirit had gone away."

During the next day all our people were invited to

attend the half-breeds' dance. I never knew before that the new year begins in midwinter. We had always counted that the year ends when the winter ends, and a new year begins with the new life in springtime.

The most exciting event of this year was the attack that the Gros Ventres made upon us just as we moved our camp upon the tableland back of the river in the spring. We had plenty of meat then and everybody was happy. The grass was beginning to appear and the ponies to grow fat.

One night there was a war dance. A few of our young men had planned to invade the Gros Ventre country, but it seemed that they too had been thinking of us. Everybody was interested in the proposed war party.

"Uncle, are you going too?" I eagerly asked him.

"No," he replied, with a long sigh. "It is the worst time of the year to go on the warpath. We shall have plenty of fighting this summer, as we are going to trench upon their territory in our hunts," he added.

The night was clear and pleasant. The war drum was answered by the howls of coyotes on the opposite side of the Mouse River. I was in the throng, watching the braves who were about to go out in search of glory. "I wish I were old enough; I would surely go with this party," I thought. My friend Tatanka was to go. He was several years older than I, and a hero in my eyes. I watched him as he danced with the rest until nearly midnight. Then I came back to our tepee and rolled myself in my buffalo robe and was soon lost in sleep.

Suddenly I was aroused by loud war cries. "Woo! woo! hay-ay! hay-ay! U we do! U we do!" I jumped upon my feet, snatched my bow and arrows, and rushed out of the tepee, frantically yelling as I went.

"Stop! stop!" screamed Uncheedah, and caught me by my long hair.

By this time the Gros Ventres had encircled our camp, sending volleys of arrows and bullets into our midst. The women were digging ditches in which to put their children.

My uncle was foremost in the battle. The Sioux bravely withstood the assault, although several of our men had already fallen. Many of the enemy were killed in the field around our tepees. The Sioux at last got their ponies and made a counter charge, led by Oye-makasan (my uncle). They cut the Gros Ventre party in two and drove them off.

My friend Tatanka was killed. I took one of his eagle feathers, thinking I would wear it the first time that I ever went upon the warpath. I thought I would give anything for the opportunity to go against the Gros Ventres, because they killed my friend. The war songs, the wailing for the dead, the howling of the dogs were intolerable to me. Soon after this we broke up our camp and departed for new scenes.

IX

Wild Harvests

WHEN our people lived in Minnesota, a good part of their natural subsistence was furnished by the wild rice that grew abundantly in all of that region. Around the shores and all over some of the innumerable lakes of the Land of Sky-blue Water was this wild cereal found. Indeed, some of the watery fields in those days might be compared in extent and fruitfulness with the fields of wheat on Minnesota's magnificent farms today.

The wild-rice harvesters came in groups of fifteen to twenty families to a lake, depending upon the size of the harvest. Some of the Indians hunted buffalo upon the prairie at this season, but there were more who preferred to go to the lakes to gather wild rice, fish, and berries, and hunt the deer. There was an abundance of waterfowl among the grain; no season of the year was happier than this.

The campground was usually an attractive spot, with shade and cool breezes off the water. The people, while they pitched their tepees upon the heights, if possible, for the sake of a good outlook, actually lived in their canoes upon the placid waters. The happiest of all, perhaps, were the young maidens, who were all day long in their canoes, in twos or threes, and when tired of gathering the wild cereal, would sit in the boats doing their needlework.

These maidens learned to imitate the calls of the different waterfowl as a sort of signal to the members of a group. Even the old women and the boys adopted signals so that while the population of the village was lost to sight in a thick field of wild rice, a meeting could be arranged without calling anyone by his or her own name. It was a great convenience for those young men who sought opportunity to meet certain maidens.

August is the harvest month. There were many preliminary feasts of fish, ducks, and venison, and offerings in honor of the Water Chief so that there might not be any drowning accident during the harvest. The preparation consisted of a series of feasts and offerings for many days, while women and men were making birch canoes, for nearly every member of the family must be provided with one for this occasion. The blueberry and huckleberry picking also preceded the rice gathering.

On the appointed day all the canoes were carried to the shore and placed upon the water with prayer and propitiatory offerings. Each family took possession of the allotted field and tied all the grain in bundles of convenient size, allowing it to stand for a few days. Then they again entered the lake, assigning two persons to each canoe. One manipulated the paddle, while the foremost one gently drew the heads of each bundle toward him and gave it a few strokes with a light rod. This caused the rice to fall into the bottom of the craft. The field was traversed in this manner back and forth until finished.

This was the pleasantest and easiest part of the harvest toil. The real work was when they prepared the rice for use. First of all, it must be made perfectly dry. They would spread it upon buffalo robes and mats, and sometimes upon layers of coarse swamp grass, and dry it in the sun. If time was short, they would make a scaffold and spread upon it a certain thickness of the green grass and afterward the rice. Under this a fire was made, taking care that the grass did not catch fire.

When all the rice is gathered and dried, the hulling begins. A round hole is dug about two feet deep and the same in diameter. Then the rice is heated over a fireplace and emptied into the hole while it is hot. A young man, having washed his feet and put on a new pair of moccasins, treads upon it until all is hulled. The women then pour it upon a robe and begin to shake it so that the chaff will be separated by the wind. Some of the rice is browned before being hulled.

During the hulling time there were prizes offered to the young men who could hull quickest and best. There were sometimes from twenty to fifty youths dancing with their feet in these holes.

Pretty moccasins were brought by shy maidens to the youths of their choice, asking them to hull rice. There were daily entertainments that deserved some such name as hulling bee.

When all the rice was prepared for the table, the

matter of storing it must be determined. Caches were dug by each family in a concealed spot and carefully lined with dry grass and bark. Here they left their surplus stores for a time of need. Our people were very ingenious in covering up all traces of the hidden food. A common trick was to build a fire on top of the mound. As much of the rice as could be carried conveniently was packed in parfleches, or cases made of rawhide, and brought back with us to our village.

After all, the wild Indians could not be justly termed improvident when their manner of life is taken into consideration. They let nothing go to waste and labored incessantly during the summer and fall to lay up provision for the inclement season. Berries of all kinds were industriously gathered and dried in the sun. Even the wild cherries were pounded up, stones and all, made into small cakes, and dried for use in soups and for mixing with the pounded jerked meat and fat to form a much-prized Indian delicacy.

Out on the prairie in July and August, the women were wont to dig *teepsinna*[1] with sharpened sticks, and many a bag full was dried and put away. It is starchy but solid, with a sweetish taste, and is very fattening. It can be eaten raw or stewed and is always kept in a dried state, except when it is first dug.

The primitive housekeeper exerted herself much to secure a variety of appetizing dishes; she even robbed the field mouse and the muskrat to accom-

[1]The Dakota ate this bulbous root, which grows on the high prairies at the beginning of each summer.

plish her end. The tiny mouse gathers for her winter use several excellent kinds of food. Among these is a wild bean, which equals in flavor any domestic bean that I have ever tasted. Her storehouse is usually under a peculiar mound, which the untrained eye would be unable to distinguish from an anthill. There are many pockets underneath, into which she industriously gathers the harvest of the summer.

She is fortunate if the quick eye of a native woman does not detect her hiding place. About the month of September, while traveling over the prairie, a woman is occasionally observed to halt suddenly and waltz around a suspected mound. Finally the pressure of her heels causes a place to give way, and she settles contentedly down to rob the poor mouse.

The different kinds of beans are put away in different pockets, but it is the *oomenechah* she wants. The field mouse loves this savory vegetable, for she always gathers it more than any other. There is also some of the white star-like *manakcahkcah*, the root of the wild lily. This is a good medicine and good to eat.

When our people were gathering wild rice, they always watched for another plant that grows in the muddy bottom of lakes and ponds. It is a white bulb about the size of an ordinary onion. This is stored away by the muskrats in their houses by the waterside, and there is often a bushel or more of the *psinchinchah* to be found within.

I have referred to the opportunities for courting upon wild rice fields. Indian courtship is peculiar in many respects; but when you study their daily life, you will see the philosophy of their etiquette of love-making. There was no parlor courtship; the life was largely out-of-doors, which was very favorable to the young men.

In a nomadic life where the female members of the family have entire control of domestic affairs, the work is divided among them all. Very often the bringing of the wood and water devolves upon the young maids, and the spring or the woods becomes the battleground for love's warfare. The nearest water may be some distance from the camp, which is all the better. Sometimes, too, there is no wood to be had; and in that case, one would see the young women scattered all over the prairie, gathering buffalo chips for fuel.

This is the way the red men go about to induce the aboriginal maids to listen to their suit. As soon as the youth had returned from the warpath or the chase, he puts on his porcupine-quill embroidered moccasins and leggings and folds his best robe about him. He brushes his long, glossy hair with a brush made from the tail of a porcupine, perfumes it with scented grass or leaves, and then arranges it in two plaits with an otter skin or some other ornament. If he is a warrior, he adds an eagle feather or two.

If he chooses to ride, he takes his best pony. He jumps upon its bare back, simply throwing a part of his robe under him to serve as a saddle and holding the end of a lariat tied about the animal's neck. He guides him altogether by the motions of his body.

These wily ponies seem to enter into the spirit of the occasion and very often capture the eyes of the maid by their graceful movements, in perfect obedience to their master.

The general custom is for the young men to pull their robes over their heads, leaving only a slit to look through. Sometimes the same is even done by the maiden—especially in public courtship.

He approaches the girl while she is coming from the spring. He takes up his position directly in her path. If she is in a hurry or does not care to stop, she goes around him; but if she is willing to stop and listen, she puts down on the ground the vessel of water she is carrying.

Very often at the first meeting the maiden does not know who her lover is. He does not introduce himself immediately but waits until a second meeting. Sometimes she does not see his face at all, and then she will try to find out who he is and what he looks like before they meet again. If he is not a desirable suitor, she will go with her chaperon and end the affair there.

There are times when maidens go in twos, and then there must be two young men to meet them.

There is some courtship in the nighttime, either in the early part of the evening, on the outskirts of dances and other public affairs, or after everybody is supposed to be asleep. This is the secret courtship. The youth may pull up the tent pins just back of his sweetheart and speak with her during the night. He must be a smart young man to do that undetected, for the grandmother, the maiden's chaperon, is usually all ears.

Elopements are common. There are many reasons for a girl or a youth to defer their wedding. It may be from personal pride of one or both. The wellborn are married publicly, and many things are given away in their honor. The maiden may desire to attend a certain number of maidens' feasts before marrying. The youth may be poor, or he may wish to achieve another honor before surrendering to a woman.

Sometimes a youth is so infatuated with a maiden that he will follow her to any part of the country, even after their respective bands have separated for the season. I knew of one such case. Patah Tankah had courted a distant relative of my uncle for a long time. There seemed to be some objection to him on the part of the girl's parents, although the girl was willing.

The large camp had been broken up for the fall hunt, and my uncle's band went one way, while the young man's family went in the other direction. After three days' traveling, we came to a good hunting ground and made camp. One evening, somebody saw the young man. He had been following his sweetheart and sleeping out-of-doors all that time, although the nights were already frosty and cold. He met her every day in secret, and she brought him food. But, he would not come near the tepee. Finally her people yielded, and she went back with him to his band.

X

A Meeting on the Plains

WE WERE encamped at one time on the Souris or Mouse River, a tributary of the Assiniboine. The buffaloes were still plenty; hence we were living on the fat of the land. One afternoon a scout came in with the announcement that a body of United States troops was approaching! This report, of course, caused much uneasiness among our people.

A council was held immediately, in the course of which the scout was put through a rigid examination. Before a decision had been reached, another scout came in from the field. He declared that the moving train reported as a body of troops was in reality a train of Canadian carts.

The two reports differed so widely that it was deemed wise to send out more runners to observe this moving body closely and ascertain definitely its character. These soon returned with the positive information that the Canadians were at hand, "for," said they, "there are no bright metals in the moving train to send forth flashes of light. The separate bodies are short, like carts with ponies, and not like the long, four-wheeled wagon drawn by four or six mules that the soldiers use. They are not buffaloes, and they cannot be mounted troops because the individual bodies are too long for that. Besides, the soldiers usually have their chief, with his guards, leading the train; and the little chiefs are also separated from the main body and ride at one side!"

From these observations it was concluded that we were soon to meet with the *bois brûlés,* as the French call their mixed-bloods, presumably from the color of their complexions. Some say that they are named from the burned forests, which, as woodcutters, they are accustomed to leave behind them. Two or three hours later, at about sunset, our ears began to distinguish the peculiar music that always accompanied a moving train of their carts. It is like the grunting and squealing of many animals and is because the wheels and all other parts of these vehicles are made of wood.

They stopped a little way from our camp, upon a grassy plain, and the ponies were made to wheel their clumsy burdens into a perfect circle, the shafts being turned inward. Thus was formed a sort of barricade— quite a usual and necessary precaution in their nomadic and adventurous life. Within this circle the tents were pitched, and many cheerful fires were soon kindled.

Our chief and his principal warriors briefly conferred with the strangers, and it was understood by both parties that no thought of hostilities lurked in the minds of either.

After having observed the exchange of presents that always follows a peace council, there were friendly and hospitable feasts in both camps. The *bois brûlés* had been long away from any fort or trading post, and it so happened that their inevitable whiskey keg was almost empty. They had diluted the few gills remaining with several large kettles full of water. In order to have any sort of offensive taste, it was necessary to add cayenne pepper and a little gentian.

Our men were treated to this concoction; and seeing that two or three of the half-breeds pretended to become intoxicated, our braves followed their example. They made the night intolerable with their shouts and singing until past midnight, when gradually all disturbance ceased.

Suddenly the loud report of a gun stirred those who were sleeping. Many more reports were heard in quick succession, all coming from the camp of the *bois brûlés*. Every man among the Sioux sprang to his feet, weapon in hand, and many ran toward their ponies. But there was one significant point about the untimely firing of the guns—they were all directed heavenward! One of our old men, who understood better than anyone else the manners of half-breeds, thus proclaimed at the top of his voice: "Let the people sleep! This that we have heard is the announcement of a boy's advent into the world! It is their custom to introduce with gunpowder a newborn boy!"

Again quiet was restored in the neighboring camps, and for a time the night reigned undisturbed. But scarcely had we fallen into a sound sleep when we were for the second time rudely aroused by the firing of guns and the yelling of warriors. This time it was discovered that almost all the ponies, including those of our neighbors, had been stealthily driven off by horse thieves of another tribe.

These Blackfeet miscreants were adept in their profession, for they had accomplished their purpose with much skill, almost under the very eyes of the foe; and had it not been for the invincible superstition of Slow Dog, they would have met with complete success. As it was, they caused us no little trouble and anxiety, but after a hot pursuit of a whole day, and with the assistance of the half-breeds, our horses were recaptured.

Slow Dog was one of those Indians who are filled with conceit, and boasting loudly their pretensions as medicine men, without any success, only bring upon themselves an unnecessary amount of embarrassment and ridicule. Yet there is one quality always possessed by such persons, among a savage people as elsewhere—namely, great perseverance and tenacity in their self-assertion. So the blessing of ignorance kept Slow Dog always cheerful; and he seemed, if anything, to derive some pleasure from the endless insinuations and ridicule of the people!

Now Slow Dog had loudly proclaimed, on the night before this event, that he had received the warning of a bad dream, in which he had seen all the tribe's ponies stampeded and driven westward.

"But who cares for Slow Dog's dream?" said everybody. "None of the really great medicine men have had any such visions!"

Therefore, our little community, given as they were to superstition, anticipated no special danger. It is true that when the first scout reported the approach of troops, some of the people had weakened and said to one another:

"After all, perhaps poor Slow Dog may be right; perhaps we were always too ready to laugh at him!"

However, this feeling quickly passed away when the jovial Canadians arrived, and the old man was left alone to brood upon his warning.

He was faithful to his dream. During all the hilarity of the feast and the drinking of the mock whiskey, he acted as self-constituted sentinel. Finally, when everybody else had succumbed to sleep, he gathered together several broken and discarded lariats of various materials—leather, buffalo's hair, and horse's hair. Having lengthened this variegated rope with innumerable knots, he fastened one end of it around the neck of his old war horse and tied the other to his wrist. Instead of sleeping inside the tent as usual, he rolled himself in a buffalo robe and lay down in its shadow. From this place he watched until the moon had disappeared behind the western horizon; and just as the gray dawn began to appear in the east, his eyes were attracted to what seemed to be a dog moving among the picketed ponies. Upon a closer scrutiny, he saw that its actions were unnatural.

"Toka ahe do! Toka ahe do!" (the enemy! the enemy!) exclaimed Slow Dog. With a war whoop he sprang toward the intruder, who rose up and leaped

upon the back of Slow Dog's war steed. He had cut the hobble,[1] as well as the device of the old medicine man.

The Sioux now bent his bow to shoot, but it was too late. The other quickly dodged behind the animal, and from under its chest he sent a deadly arrow to Slow Dog's bosom. Then he remounted the pony and set off at full speed after his comrades.

As the Sioux braves responded to the alarm and passed by the daring old warrior in pursuit of their enemies, who had stampeded most of the loose ponies, the old man cried out: "I, brave Slow Dog, who have so often made a path for you on the field of battle, am now to make one to the land of spirits!"

So speaking, the old man died. The Sioux were joined in the chase by the friendly mixed-bloods, and in the end the Blackfeet were compelled to pay dearly for the blood of the poor old man.

On that beautiful morning all nature seemed brilliant and smiling, but the Sioux were mourning and wailing for the death of one who been an object of ridicule most of his life. They appreciated the part that Slow Dog had played in this last event, and his memory was honored by all the tribe.

[1]hobble: a tie that holds two legs of a horse together to keep the animal from running away.

XI

An Adventurous Journey

I T MUST now be about thirty years since our long journey in search of new hunting grounds, from the Assiniboine River to the upper Missouri. The buffalo, formerly so abundant between the two rivers, had begun to shun their usual haunts, on account of the great numbers of Canadian half-breeds in that part of the country. There was also the first influx of English sportsmen, whose wholesale methods of destruction wrought such havoc with the herds. These seemingly intelligent animals correctly prophesied to the natives the approach of the paleface.

As we had anticipated, we found game very scarce as we traveled slowly across the vast plains. There were only herds of antelope and sometimes flocks of waterfowl, with here and there a lonely bull straggling aimlessly along. At first our party was small, but as we proceeded on our way, we fell in with some of the western bands of Sioux and Assiniboines, who are close connections.

Each day the camp was raised and marched from ten to twenty miles. One might wonder how such a cavalcade would look in motion. The only vehicles were the primitive travois drawn by ponies and large Eskimo dogs. A large basket suspended between the poles, just above the ground, supplied a place for goods and a safe nest for the babies, or an occasional helpless old woman. Most of our effects were carried by pack ponies, and an Indian packer excels all others in quickness and dexterity.

The train was nearly a mile long, headed by a number of old warriors on foot, who carried the filled pipe and decided when and where to stop. A very warm day made much trouble for the women who had charge of the moving household. The pack dogs were especially unmanageable. They would become very thirsty and run into the water with their loads. The scolding of the women, the singing of the old men, and the yelps of the Indian dudes made our progress a noisy one, and like that of a town in motion rather than an ordinary company of travelers.

This journey of ours was not without its exciting episodes. My uncle had left the main body and gone off to the south with a small party, as he was accustomed to do every summer, to seek revenge of some sort on the whites for all injuries that they had inflicted upon our family. This time he met with a company of soldiers between Fort Totten and Fort Berthold, in North Dakota. Somehow, these seven Indians surprised the troopers in broad daylight while eating their dinner and captured the whole outfit, including nearly all their mules and one white horse, with such of their provisions as they cared to carry back with them. No doubt these soldiers reported at the fort that they had been attacked by a large party of Indians, and I dare say some promotions rewarded their tale of brave defense! However, the facts are just as I have stated them. My uncle brought home the white horse, and the fine Spanish mules were taken by the others. Among the things they brought back with them were several loaves of raised bread, the first I had ever seen and a great curiosity. We called it *aguayape tachangu,* or lung bread, from its spongy consistency.

Although when a successful war party returns with so many trophies, there is usually much dancing and hilarity, there was almost nothing of the kind on this occasion. The reason was that the enemy made little resistance; and then there was our old tradition with regard to the whites that there is no honor in conquering them, as they fight only under compulsion.

It was upon this journey that a hunter performed the feat of shooting an arrow through three antelopes. This statement may perhaps be doubted, yet I can vouch for its authenticity. He was not alone at the time, and those who were with him are reliable witnesses. The animals were driven upon a marshy peninsula, where they were crowded together and almost helpless. Many were dispatched with knives and arrows; and a man by the name of Grey-foot, who was large and tall and an extraordinarily fine hunter, actually sent his arrow through three of them. This feat was not accomplished by mere strength, for it requires a great deal of skill as well.

A misfortune occurred near the river, which deprived us of one of our best young men. There was no other man, except my own uncle, for whom I had at that time so great an admiration. Very strangely, as it appeared to me, he bore a Christian name. He was commonly called Jacob. I did not discover how he came by such a curious and apparently meaningless name until after I had returned to the United States. His father had been converted by one of the early missionaries, before the Minnesota massacre in 1862, and the boy had been baptized Jacob. He was an ideal woodsman and hunter, and really a hero in my eyes. He was one of the party of seven who had attacked and put to rout the white soldiers.

The trouble arose thus. Jacob had taken from the soldiers two good mules, and soon afterward we fell in with some Canadian half-breeds who were desirous of trading for them. However, the young man would not trade; he was not at all disposed to part with his fine mules. A certain one of the mixed-bloods was intent upon getting possession of these animals by fair or unfair means. He invited Jacob to dinner and treated him to whiskey, but the Indian youth declined the liquor. The half-breed pretended to take this refusal as an insult. He seized his gun and shot his guest dead.

In a few minutes the scene was one of almost unprecedented excitement. Every adult Indian, female as well as male, was bent upon invading the camp of the *bois brûlés*, to destroy the murderer. The confusion was made yet more intolerable by the wailing of the women and the singing of death songs.

Our number was now ten to one of the half-breeds.

Within the circle formed by their carts, they prepared for a desperate resistance. The hills about their little encampment were covered with warriors, ready to pounce upon them at the signal of their chief.

The older men, however, were discussing in council what should be demanded of the half-breeds. It was determined that the murderer must be given up to us, to be punished according to the laws of the plains. If, however, they should refuse to give him up, the mode of attack decided upon was to build a fire around the offenders and thus stampede their horses, or at the least divide their attention. Meanwhile, the braves were to make a sudden onset.

Just then a piece of white, newly tanned deerskin was hoisted up in the center of the *bois brûlé* encampment. It was a flag of truce. One of their number approached the council lodge, unarmed and making the sign for a peaceful communication. He was admitted to the council, which was still in session, and offered to give up the murderer. It was also proposed, as an alternative, that the murderer give everything he had to the parents of the murdered man.

The parents were allowed no voice whatever in the discussion that followed, for they were regarded as incompetent judges, under the circumstances. It was finally decreed by the council that the man's life should be spared but that he must be exposed to the indignity of a public whipping and resign all his earthly possessions to the parents of his victim. This sentence was carried into effect.

In our nomadic life there were a few unwritten laws by which our people were governed. There was a council, a police force, and an executive officer, who was not always the chief but a member of the tribe appointed to this position for a given number of days. There were also the wise old men who were constantly in attendance at the council lodge and acted as judges in the rare event of the commission of a crime.

This simple government of ours was supported by the issue of little sticks about five inches long. There were a hundred or so of these, and they were distributed every few days by the police or soldiers, who kept account of them. Whoever received one of these sticks must return it within five or ten days, with a load of provisions. If one was held beyond the stipulated time, the police would call the delinquent warrior to account. In case he did not respond, they could come and destroy his tent or take away his weapons. When all the sticks had been returned, they were then reissued to other men; and so the council lodge was supported.

It was the custom that no man who had not distinguished himself upon the warpath could destroy the home of another. This was a necessary qualification for the office of an Indian policeman. These policemen must also oversee the hunt, lest some individuals should be well provided with food while others were in want. No man might hunt independently. The game must be carefully watched by the game scouts and the discovery of a herd reported at once to the council,

Dr. Charles Alexander Eastman, Ohiyesa,
Julius D. Katzieff, oil on canvas

Courtesy Hood Museum of Art, Dartmouth College, Gift of Class of 1887

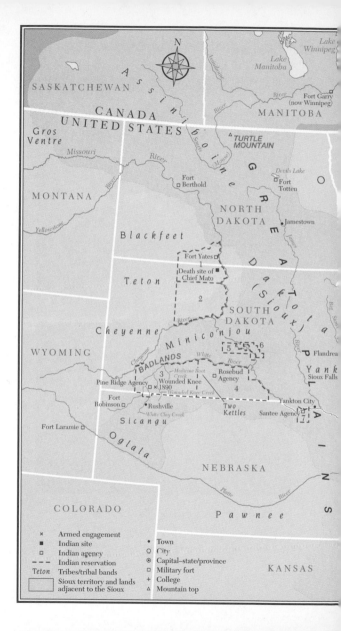

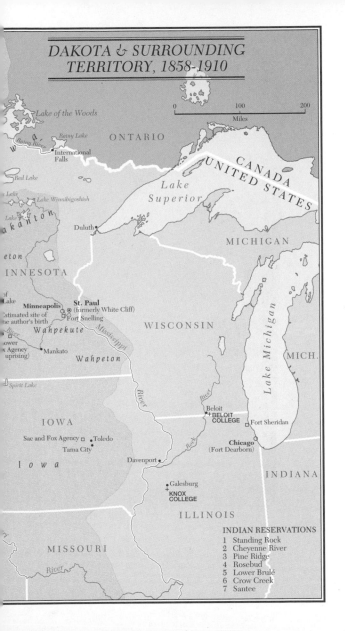

DAKOTA & SURROUNDING TERRITORY, 1858–1910

0   100   200

Miles

Lake of the Woods

Rainy River

Rainy Lake

International Falls

ONTARIO

CANADA

UNITED STATES

Red Lake

Lake Winnibigoshish

Lake

Lake Superior

Duluth

MICHIGAN

akanton

eton

MINNESOTA

of
Lake

Minneapolis   St. Paul
(formerly White Cliff)
Estimated site of   Fort Snelling
the author's birth

Wahpekute

Mississippi

WISCONSIN

Lake Michigan

MICH.

ower
x Agency
uprising)

Mankato

Wahpeton

Spirit Lake

IOWA

Sac and Fox Agency   Toledo
Tama City

River

Rock River

Beloit
BELOIT
COLLEGE

Fort Sheridan

I o w a

Davenport

Chicago
(Fort Dearborn)

INDIANA

Galesburg
KNOX
COLLEGE

ILLINOIS

MISSOURI

River

INDIAN RESERVATIONS

1   Standing Rock
2   Cheyenne River
3   Pine Ridge
4   Rosebud
5   Lower Brulé
6   Crow Creek
7   Santee

59.

Nancy
N. E. - halfbred.
Eastman -

Previously unpublished pencil sketches of Mary Nancy Eastman,
Charles Eastman's mother, by Frank B. Mayer, 1851

Indian Mode of Traveling, *Seth Eastman, oil on canvas, 1869*

Courtesy Architect of the Capitol, Collection of the U.S. House of Representatives

Rice Gatherers, *Seth Eastman, oil on canvas, 1867*

Courtesy Architect of the Capitol, Collection of the U.S. House of Representatives

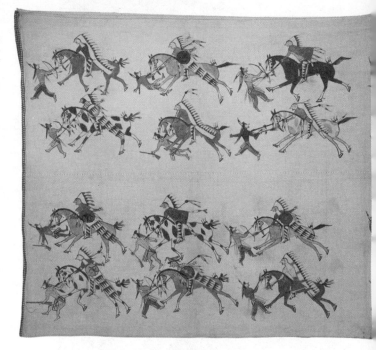

Wahpeton Dakota cotton tepee liner

Courtesy National Museum of the American Indian, Smithsonian Institution

Eastern Sioux pipe bowl,
ca. 1880

Courtesy The Detroit Institute of Arts

Execution by hanging of Dakota Indians after Uprising of 1862

Courtesy Minnesota Historical Society

Arapaho Ghost Dance shirt

Courtesy National Museum of American History, Smithsonian Institution

Indian Sugar Camp, *Seth Eastman, watercolor*

Dog Dance of the Dakotas, *from* American Aboriginal Portfolio, *Seth Eastman, 1849*

Courtesy The Newberry Library

105

Ball Play of the Dakota (Sioux) Indians, *from* American Aboriginal Portfolio, *Seth Eastman*

Courtesy The Newberry Library

Hunting the Buffalo in Winter, *Seth Eastman, watercolor*

Courtesy Ayer Collection, The Newberry Library

after which the time and manner of the hunt were publicly announced.

I well recall how the herald announced the near approach of buffaloes. It was supposed that if the little boys could trip up the old man while going on his rounds, the success of the hunt was assured. The oftener he was tripped, the more successful it would be! The signal or call for buffaloes was a peculiar whistle. As soon as the herald appeared, all the boys would give the whistle and follow in crowds after the poor old man. Of course he tried to avoid them, but they were generally too quick for him.

There were two kinds of scouts, for hunting and for war. In one sense every Indian was a scout, but some were especially appointed to serve for a certain length of time. An Indian might hunt every day, besides the regularly organized hunt, but he was liable to punishment at any time. If he could kill a solitary buffalo or deer without disturbing the herd, it was allowed. He might also hunt small game.

In the movable town under such a government as this, there was apt to be inconvenience and actual suffering, since a great body of people was supported only by the daily hunt. Hence there was a constant disposition to break up into smaller parties, in order to obtain food more easily and freely. Yet the wise men of the Dakotas would occasionally form large bands of from 2,000 to 5,000 people, who camped and moved about together for a period of some months. It is apparent that so large a body could not be supplied easily with the necessaries of life; but, on the other hand, our enemies respected such a gathering! Of course the nomadic government would do its utmost to hold together as long as possible. The police did all they could to keep in check those parties who were intent upon stealing away.

There were many times, however, when individual bands and even families were justified in seeking to separate themselves from the rest, in order to gain a better support. It was chiefly by reason of this food question that the Indians never established permanent towns or organized themselves into a more formidable nation.

There was a sad misfortune that, although it happened many generations ago, was familiarly quoted among us. A certain band became very independent and unruly; they went so far as to willfully disobey the orders of the general government. The police were directed to punish the leader severely; whereupon the rest defended him and resisted the police. But the latter were competent to enforce their authority, and as a result the entire band was annihilated.

One day, as we were following along the bank of the upper Missouri, there appeared to be a great disturbance at the head of the cavalcade—so much so that we thought our people had been attacked by a war party of the Crows or some of the hostile tribes of that region. In spite of the danger, even the women and children hurried forward to join the men—that is to say, as many as were not upon the hunt. Most of the warriors were out, as usual, and only the large boys and the old men were traveling with the women and their domestic effects and little ones.

As we approached the scene of action, we heard loud shouts and the report of firearms; but our party was scattered along for a considerable distance, and all was over before we could reach the spot. It was a great grizzly bear who had been bold enough to oppose, single-handed, the progress of several hundred Indians. The council men, who usually walked a little in advance of the train, were the first to meet the bear, and he was probably deceived by the sight of this advance body and thus audaciously defied them.

Among these council men—all retired chiefs and warriors whose ardent zeal had long been cooled and whose present duties were those of calm deliberation for their people's welfare—there were two old, distinguished war chiefs. Each of these men still carried his war lance, wrapped up in decorated buckskin. As the bear advanced boldly toward them, the two old men promptly threw off their robes—an evidence that there still lurked within their breasts the spirit of chivalry and ready courage. Spear in hand, they both sprang forward to combat with the ferocious animal, taking up their positions about ten feet apart.

As they had expected, the fearful beast, after getting up on his haunches and growling savagely, came forward with widely opened jaws. He fixed his eyes upon the left-hand man, who was ready to meet him with uplifted spear, but with one stroke of his powerful paw, the weapon was sent to the ground. At the same moment the right-hand man dealt him a stab that penetrated the grizzly's side.

The bear uttered a groan not unlike that of a man and seized the spear so violently that its owner was thrown to the ground. As the animal drew the lance from its body, the first man, having recovered his own, stabbed him with it on the other side. Upon this, he turned and knocked the old man down and again endeavored to extract the spear.

By this time all the dogs and men were at hand. Many arrows and balls were sent into the tough hide of the bear. Yet he would probably have killed both his assailants, had it not been for the active small dogs who were constantly upon his heels and annoying him. A deadly rifle shot at last brought him down.

The old men were badly bruised and torn, but the both of them recovered. From that day on, they bore the quite high-sounding titles of Fought-the-Bear and Conquered-the-Grizzly.

XII

First Impressions of Civilization

I WAS scarcely old enough to know anything definite about the Big Knives, as we called the white men, when the terrible Minnesota massacre broke up our home and I was carried into exile. I have already told how I was adopted into the family of my father's younger brother when my father was betrayed and imprisoned. We supposed that he had shared the fate of those executed at Mankato, Minnesota.

Now, the savage philosophers looked upon vengeance in the field of battle as a lofty virtue. To avenge the death of a relative or of a dear friend was considered a great deed. My uncle, accordingly, had spared no pains to instill into my young mind the obligation to avenge the death of my father and my older brothers. Already I looked eagerly forward to the day when I should find an opportunity to carry out his teachings. Meanwhile, he himself went upon the warpath and returned with scalps every summer. So it may be imagined how I felt toward the Big Knives!

On the other hand, I had heard marvelous things of this people. In some things we despised them; in others we regarded them as *wakan* (mysterious), a race whose power bordered upon the supernatural. I learned that they had made a "fireboat." I could not understand how they could unite two elements that cannot exist together. I thought the water would put out the fire, and the fire would consume the boat if it had the shadow of a chance. This was to me a preposterous thing! But when I was told that the Big Knives had created a "fireboat-walks-on-mountains" (a locomotive), it was too much to believe.

"Why," declared my informant, "those who saw this monster move said that it flew from mountain to mountain when it seemed to be excited. They said also that it carried a thunderbird, for they heard his usual war whoop as the creature sped along!"

Several warriors had observed from a distance one of the first trains on the Northern Pacific and had gained an exaggerated impression of the wonders of the paleface. They had seen it go over a bridge that spanned a deep ravine, and it seemed to them that it jumped from one bank to the other. I confess that the story almost quenched my ardor and bravery.

Two or three young men were talking together about this fearful invention.

"However," said one, "I understand that this fireboat-walks-on-mountains cannot move except on the track made for it."

Although a boy is not expected to join in the conversation of his elders, I ventured to ask: "Then it cannot chase us into any rough country?"

"No, it cannot do that" was the reply, which I heard with a great deal of relief.

St. Paul & Sioux City locomotive, 1870, an example of "fireboat-walks-on-mountains"

Courtesy Minnesota Historical Society

Dakota Indians drying meat, 1870

Courtesy Minnesota Historical Society

I had seen guns and various other things brought to us by the French Canadians, so that I had already some notion of the supernatural gifts of the white man; but I had never before heard such tales as I listened to that morning. It was said that they had bridged the Missouri and Mississippi Rivers and that they made immense houses of stone and brick piled on top of one another until they were as high as high hills. My brain was puzzled with these things for many a day. Finally I asked my uncle why the Great Mystery gave such power to the *Washechu* (the rich)—sometimes we called them by this name—and not to us Dakotas.

"For the same reason," he answered, "that he gave to Duta the skill to make fine bows and arrows, and to Wachesne no skill to make anything."

"And why do the Big Knives increase so much more in number than the Dakotas?" I continued.

"It has been said, and I think it must be true, that they have larger families than we do. I went into the house of an *Eashecha* (a German), and I counted no less than nine children. The eldest of them could not have been over fifteen. When my grandfather first visited them, down at the mouth of the Mississippi, they were comparatively few; later my father visited their Great Father at Washington, and they had already spread over the whole country.

"Certainly they are a heartless nation. They have made some of their people servants—yes, slaves! We have never believed in keeping slaves, but it seems that these *Washechu* do! It is our belief that they painted their servants black a long time ago, to tell them from the rest, and now the slaves have children born to them of the same color!

"The greatest object of their lives seems to be to acquire possessions—to be rich. They desire to possess the whole world. For thirty years they were trying to entice us to sell them our land. Finally the outbreak gave them all, and we have been driven away from our beautiful country.

"They are a wonderful people. They have divided the day into hours, like the moons of the year. In fact, they measure everything. Not one of them would let so much as a turnip go from his field unless he received full value for it. I understand that their great men make a feast and invite many, but when the feast is over, the guests are required to pay for what they have eaten before leaving the house. I myself saw at White Cliff (the name given to St. Paul, Minnesota) a man who kept a bass drum and a bell to call people to his table; but when he got them in, he would make them pay for the food!

"I am also informed," said my uncle, "but this I hardly believe, that their Great Chief (president) compels every man to pay him for the land he lives upon and all his personal goods—even for his own existence—every year!" (This was his idea of taxation.) "I am sure we could not live under such a law.

"When the outbreak occurred, we thought that our opportunity had come, for we had learned that the

Big Knives were fighting among themselves, on account of a dispute over their slaves. It was said that the Great Chief had allowed slaves in one part of the country and not in another, so there was jealousy, and they fought it out. We don't know how true this was.

"There were some praying-men who came to us some time before the trouble arose. They observed every seventh day as a holy day. On that day they met in a house that they had built for that purpose, to sing, pray, and speak of their Great Mystery. I was never in one of these meetings. I understand that they had a large book from which they read. By all accounts they were very different from all other white men we have known, for these never observed any such day, and we never knew them to pray, neither did they ever tell us of their Great Mystery.

"In war they have leaders and war chiefs of different grades. The common warriors are driven forward like a herd of antelope to face the foe. It is on account of this manner of fighting—from compulsion and not from personal bravery—that we count no *coup* on them. A lone warrior can do much harm to a large army of them in a bad country." It was this talk that gave me my first clear idea of the white man.

I was almost fifteen years old when my uncle presented me with a flintlock gun. The possession of the "mysterious iron," and the explosive dirt, or "pulverized coal," as it is called, filled me with new thoughts. All the war songs that I had ever heard from childhood came back to me with their heroes. It seemed as if I were an entirely new being—the boy had become a man!

"I am now old enough," said I to myself, "and I must beg my uncle to take me with him on his next warpath. I shall soon be able to avenge the blood of my father and my brothers."

I had already begun to invoke the blessing of the Great Mystery. Scarcely a day passed that I did not offer up some of my game so that he might not be displeased with me. My people saw very little of me during the day, for in solitude I found the strength I needed. I groped about in the wilderness and determined to assume my position as a man. My boyish ways were departing, and a sullen dignity and composure were taking their place.

The thought of love did not hinder my ambitions. I had a vague dream of some day courting a pretty maiden, after I had made my reputation and won the eagle feathers. One day, when I was away on the daily hunt, two strangers from the United States visited our camp. They had boldly ventured across the northern border. They were Indians but clad in the white man's garments. It was as well that I was absent with my gun.

My father, accompanied by an Indian guide, after many days' searching had found us at last. He had been imprisoned at Davenport, Iowa, with those who took part in the massacre or in the battles following, and he was taught in prison and converted by the pioneer missionaries, Drs. Williamson and Riggs. He was under sentence of death but was among the number against whom no direct evidence was found and who were finally pardoned by President Lincoln.[1]

When he was released and returned to the new reservation upon the Missouri River, he soon became convinced that life on a government reservation meant physical and moral degradation. Therefore he determined, with several others, to try the white man's way of gaining a livelihood. They accordingly left the agency against the persuasions of the agent, renounced all government assistance, and took land under the United States Homestead law,[2] on the Big Sioux River. After he had made his home there, he desired to seek his lost child. It was then a dangerous undertaking to cross the line, but his Christian love prompted him to do it. He secured a good guide and found his way in time through the vast wilderness.

As for me, I little dreamed of anything unusual to happen on my return. As I approached our camp with

[1]Three hundred three Santee Dakotas were sentenced to death for murdering settlers and soldiers. Lincoln pardoned all but forty. Many Lightnings, Eastman's father, was imprisoned in the Camp McClellan army barracks, Davenport, Iowa. There Dr. Thomas S. Williamson (1800-79) and Stephen R. Riggs (1812-83) converted Many Lightnings. Both Presbyterian missionaries devoted their lives to the welfare of the Santees. Riggs wrote *History of the Dakotas* (1865). An expert on the Dakota language, Riggs translated the Bible into that language and wrote *Grammar and Dictionary of the Dakota Language* (1852).

[2]Under the Homestead Act of 1862, any adult citizen or alien (who headed a family and had not fought against the Union in the Civil War) could pay $10 to file a claim to not more than 160 acres of the surveyed public domain, if the individual met government conditions.

my game on my shoulder, I had not the slightest pre-monition that I was suddenly to be hurled from my savage life into a life unknown to me hitherto.

When I appeared in sight of my father, who had patiently listened to my uncle's long account of my early life and training, he became very much excited. He was eager to embrace the child who, as he had just been informed, made it already the object of his life to avenge his father's blood. The loving father could not remain in the tepee and watch the boy coming, so he started to meet him. My uncle arose to go with his brother to insure his safety.

My face burned with the unusual excitement by the sight of a man wearing the Big Knives' clothing and coming toward me with my uncle.

"What does this mean, Uncle?"

"My boy, this is your father, my brother, whom we mourned as dead. He has come for you."

My father added: "I am glad that my son is strong and brave. Your brothers have adopted the white man's way; I came for you to learn this new way, too; and I want you to grow up a good man."

He had brought me some civilized clothing. At first, I disliked very much to wear garments made by the people I had hated so bitterly. But the thought that, after all, they had not killed my father and broth-ers reconciled me, and I put on the clothes.

In a few days we started for the States. I felt as if I were dead and traveling to the spirit land; for now all my old ideas were to give place to new ones, and my life was to be entirely different from that of the past.

Still, I was eager to see some of the wonderful inventions of the white people. When we reached Fort Totten, I gazed about me with lively interest and a quick imagination.

My father had forgotten to tell me that the fireboat-walks-on-mountains had its track at Jamestown and might appear at any moment. As I was watering the ponies, a peculiar shrilling noise pealed forth from just beyond the hills. The ponies threw back their heads and listened; then they ran snorting over the prairie. Meanwhile, I too had taken alarm. I leaped on the back of one of the ponies and dashed off at full speed. It was a clear day; I could not imagine what had caused such an unearthly noise. It seemed as if the world were about to burst in two!

I got upon a hill as the train appeared. "Oh!" I said to myself, "that is the fireboat-walks-on-mountains that I have heard about!" Then I drove back the ponies.

My father was accustomed every morning to read from his Bible and sing a stanza of a hymn. I was about very early with my gun for several mornings; but at last he stopped me as I was preparing to go out, and bade me wait.

I listened with much astonishment. The hymn contained the word *Jesus*. I did not comprehend what this meant; and my father then told me that Jesus was the Son of God who came on earth to save sinners and that it was because of him that he had sought me.

This conversation made a deep impression upon my mind.

Late in the fall we reached the citizen settlement at Flandreau, South Dakota, where my father and some others dwelt among the whites. Here my wild life came to an end, and my school days began.

PART II

From the Deep Woods to Civilization

FOREWORD

THE BOOK *Indian Boyhood,* published first in 1902 and in many subsequent editions, pictures the first of three distinct periods in the life of the writer of this book. His childhood and youth were a part of the free wilderness life of the first American—a life that is gone forever! By dint of much persuasion, the story has now been carried on from the point of that plunge into the unknown with which the first book ends, a change so abrupt and so overwhelming that the boy of fifteen "felt as if [he] were dead and traveling to the spirit land." We are now to hear of a single-hearted quest throughout eighteen years of adolescence and early maturity, for the attainment of the modern ideal of Christian culture; and again of a quarter of a century devoted to testing that hard-won standard in various fields of endeavor, partly by holding it up before his own race and partly by interpreting their racial ideals to the white man, leading in the end to a partial reaction in favor of the earlier, the simpler, perhaps the more spiritual philosophy. It is clearly impossible to tell the whole story, but much that cannot be told may be read between the lines. The broad outlines, the salient features of an uncommon experience are here set forth in the hope that they may strengthen for some readers the conception of our common humanity.

ELAINE GOODALE EASTMAN

XIII

The Way Opens

O<small>NE CAN</small> never be sure of what a day may bring to pass. At the age of fifteen, the deepening current of my life swung upon such a pivotal day, and in the twinkling of an eye its whole course was utterly changed; as if a little mountain brook should pause and turn upon itself to gather strength for the long journey toward an unknown ocean.

From childhood I was consciously trained to be a man; that was, after all, the basic thing; but after this I was trained to be a warrior and a hunter, and not to care for money or possessions, but to be in the broadest sense a public servant. After arriving at a reverent sense of the pervading presence of the Spirit and Giver of Life, and a deep consciousness of the brotherhood of man, the first thing for me to accomplish was to adapt myself perfectly to natural things—in other words, to harmonize myself with nature. To this end I was made to build a body both symmetrical and enduring—a house for the soul to live in—a sturdy house, defying the elements. I must have faith and patience; I must learn self-control and be able to maintain silence. I must do with as little as possible and start with nothing most of the time, because a true Indian always shares whatever he may possess.

I felt no hatred for our tribal foes. I looked upon them more as the college athlete regards his rivals from another college. There was no thought of destroying a nation, taking away their country, or reducing the people to servitude, for my race rather honored and bestowed gifts upon their enemies at the next peaceful meeting, until they had adopted the usages of the white man's warfare for spoliation and conquest.

There was one unfortunate thing about my early training, however; that is, I was taught never to spare a citizen of the United States, although we were on friendly terms with the Canadian white men. The explanation is simple. My people had been turned out of some of the finest country in the world, now forming the great states of Minnesota and Iowa. The Americans pretended to buy the land at ten cents an acre but never paid the price; the debt stands unpaid to this day. Because they did not pay, the Sioux protested; finally came the outbreak of 1862 in Minnesota, when many settlers were killed, and forthwith our people, such as were left alive, were driven by the troops into exile.

My father, who was among the fugitives in Canada, had been betrayed by a half-breed across the United States line, near what is now the city of Winnipeg. Some of the party were hanged at Fort Snelling, near St. Paul. We supposed and, in fact, were informed, that all were hanged. This was why my uncle, in whose family I lived, had taught me never to spare a white man from the United States.

During the summer and winter of 1871, the band of Sioux to which I belonged—a clan of Wahpetonwans, or Dwellers Among the Leaves—roamed in the upper Missouri region and along the Yellowstone River. In that year I tasted to the full the joy and plenty of wild existence. I saw buffalo, elk, and antelope in herds numbering thousands. The forests teemed with deer, and in the Badlands dwelt the Big Horns or Rocky Mountain sheep. At this period, grizzly bears were numerous and were brought into camp quite commonly, like any other game.

We frequently met and camped with the Hudson Bay half-breeds[1] in their summer hunt of the buffalo, and we were on terms of friendship with the Assiniboines and the Crees, but in frequent collision with the Blackfeet, the Gros Ventres, and the Crows. However, there were times of truce when all met in peace for a great midsummer festival and exchange of gifts. The Sioux roamed over an area nearly a thousand miles in extent. In the summer we gathered together in large numbers, but toward fall we would divide into small groups or bands and scatter for the trapping and the winter hunt. Most of us hugged the wooded river bottoms; some depended entirely upon the buffalo for food, while others, and among these my immediate kindred, hunted all kinds of game, and trapped and fished as well.

[1]Eastman probably refers to the mixed-bloods who worked for or resided near the Hudson Bay Company trading posts.

Thus I was trained thoroughly for an all-round life outdoors and for all natural emergencies. I was a good rider and a good shot with the bow and arrow, alert and alive to everything that came within my ken. I had never known nor ever expected to know any life but this.

In the winter and summer of 1872, we drifted toward the southern part of what is now Manitoba. In this wild, rolling country I rapidly matured and laid, as I supposed, the foundations of my life career, never dreaming of anything beyond this manful and honest, unhampered existence. My horse and my dog were my closest companions. I regarded them as brothers, and if there was a hereafter, I expected to meet them there. With them I went out daily into the wilderness to seek inspiration and store up strength for coming manhood. My teachers dreamed no more than I of any change in my prospects. I had now taken part in all our tribal activities except that of war and was nearly old enough to be initiated into the ritual of the warpath. The world was full of natural rivalry; I was eager for the day.

I had attained the age of fifteen years and was about to enter into and realize a man's life, as we Indians understood it, when the change came. One fine September morning as I returned from the daily hunt, there seemed to be an unusual stir and excitement as I approached our camp. I found that my father had come—he whom we thought dead at the hands of the white men.

It was a day of miracle in the deep Canadian wilderness, before the Canadian Pacific had been even dreamed of, while the Indian and the buffalo still held sway over the vast plains of Manitoba east of the Rocky Mountains. It was, perhaps, because he was my honored father that I lent my bewildered ear to his eloquent exposition of the so-called civilized life, or the way of the white man. I could not doubt my own father, so mysteriously come back to us, as it were, from the spirit land; yet there was a voice within saying to me, "A false life! a treacherous life!"

In accordance with my training, I asked few questions, although many arose in my mind. I simply tried silently to fit the new ideas like so many blocks into the pattern of my philosophy, while according to my untutored logic, some did not seem to have straight sides or square corners to fit in with the cardinal principles of eternal justice. My father had been converted by Protestant missionaries, and he gave me a totally new vision of the white man, as a religious man and a kindly one. But when he related how he had set apart every seventh day for religious duties and the worship of God, laying aside every other occupation on that day, I could not forbear exclaiming, "Father! and does he then forget God during the six days and do as he pleases?"

"Our own life, I will admit, is the best in a world of our own, such as we have enjoyed for ages," said my father. "But here is a race which has learned to weigh and measure everything, time, labor, and the results of labor, and has learned to accumulate and preserve both wealth and the records of experience for future generations. You yourselves know and use some of the wonderful inventions of the white man, such as guns and gunpowder, knives and hatchets, garments of every description, and there are thousands of other things both beautiful and useful.

"Above all, they have their Great Teacher, whom they call Jesus, and he taught them to pass on their wisdom and knowledge to all other races. It is true that they have subdued and taught many peoples, and our own must eventually bow to this law; the sooner we accept their mode of life and follow their teaching, the better it will be for us all. I have thought much on this matter, and such is my conclusion."

There was a mingling of admiration and indignation in my mind as I listened. My father's two brothers were still far from being convinced, but filial duty and affection overweighed all my prejudices. I was bound to go back with him as he desired me to do, and my grandmother and her only daughter accompanied us on the perilous journey.

The line between Canada and the United States was closely watched at this time by hostile Indians. Therefore, my father thought it best to make a dash for Devils Lake, in North Dakota, where he could get assistance if necessary. He knew Major Forbes,[2] who was in command of the military post and the agency.

[2]In 1871, William H. Forbes became the first official agent at Devils Lake.

Our guide we knew to be an unscrupulous man, who could easily betray us for a kettle of whiskey or a pony.

One of the first things I observed was my father's reading aloud from a book every morning and evening followed by a very strange song and a prayer. Although all he said was in Indian, I did not understand it fully. He apparently talked aloud to the Great Mystery, asking for safe guidance back to his home in the States. The first reading of this book of which I have any recollection was the Twenty-Third Psalm, and the first hymn he sang in my presence was to the old tune of Ortonville.[3] It was his Christian faith and devotion which was perhaps the strongest influence toward my change of heart and complete change of my purpose in life.

I think it was at our second encampment that we met a large caravan of Canadian half-breeds accompanied by a band of Northern Ojibways. As was usual with the former, they had plenty of whiskey. They were friendly enough with us, at least while sober, but the Indians were not. Father showed them his papers as a United States citizen and a letter from Major Forbes, telling of his peaceful mission, but we could not trust our ancestral enemies, the Ojibways, especially when excited with strong drink. My father was

[3]Eastman may be referring to the hymn based on Luke 22.19, the first stanza of which is "According to thy gracious word, / In meek humility, / This will I do, my dying Lord, / I will remember thee." Other hymns sung to this tune include "The Name of Jesus" and "One Altogether Lovely."

calm and diplomatic throughout, thus privately instructed me: "My son, conceal yourself in the woods; and if the worst comes, you must flee on your swift pony. Before daylight you can pass the deep woods and cross the Assiniboine River." He handed me a letter to Major Forbes. I said, "I will try," and as soon as it was dark, I hid myself, to be in readiness. Meanwhile, my father called the leading half-breeds together and told them again that he was under the protection of his government, also that the Sioux would hold them responsible if anything happened to us. Just then they discovered that another young brave and I were not to be found, which made them think that father had dispatched us to the nearest military post for help. They immediately led away their drunken comrades and made a big talk to their Ojibway friends, so that we remained undisturbed until morning.

Some days later, at the south end of Devils Lake, I left our camp early to shoot some ducks when the morning flight should begin. Suddenly, when out of sight of the others, my eye caught a slight movement in the rank grass. Instinctively I dropped and flattened myself upon the ground, but soon a quick glance behind me showed plainly the head of a brave hidden behind a bush. I waited, trying to figure out some plan of escape, yet facing the probability that I was already surrounded, until I caught sight of another head almost in front and still another to my left.

In the moments that elapsed after I fully realized

my situation, I thought of almost everything that had happened to me up to that day, of a remarkable escape from the Ojibways, of the wild pets I had had, and of my playmates in the Canadian camps whom I should never see again. I also thought with more curiosity than fear of the Great Mystery that I was so soon to enter. As these thoughts were passing through my mind, I carelessly moved and showed myself plainly to the enemy.

Suddenly, from behind the nearest bush, came the sound of my own Sioux tongue and the words, "Are you a Sioux?" Possibly my countenance may not have changed much, but certainly I grew weak with surprise and relief. As soon as I answered "Yes!" I was surrounded by a group of warriors of my tribe, who chuckled at the joke that had come so near to costing me my life, for one of them explained that he had been on the point of firing when I exposed myself so plainly that he saw I was not an Ojibway in war paint but probably a Sioux like himself.

After a variety of adventures, we arrived at the canvas city of Jamestown, then the terminal point of the Northern Pacific Railroad.[4] I was out watering the ponies when a terrific peal of thunder burst from a spotless blue sky, and indeed seemed to me to be running along the surface of the ground. The terrified

[4]In 1872, the Northern Pacific Railroad constructed a terminal at Jamestown, located on the James River in central North Dakota. Goods for the Devils Lake Agency, eighty-two miles away, were transported by wagon from Jamestown to the agency.

ponies instantly stampeded, and I confess I was not far behind them, when a monster with one fiery eye poked his head around a corner of the hill. When we reached camp, my father kindly explained, and I was greatly relieved.

It was a peaceful Indian summer day when we reached Flandreau, in Dakota Territory, the citizen Indian settlement, and found the whole community gathered together to congratulate and welcome us home.

XIV

My First School Days

IT WAS less than a month since I had been a rover and a hunter in the Manitoba wilderness, with no thoughts save those which concern the most free and natural life of an Indian. Now, I found myself standing near a rude log cabin on the edge of a narrow strip of timber, overlooking the fertile basin of the Big Sioux River. As I gazed over the rolling prairie land, all I could see was that it met the sky at the horizon line. It seemed to me vast and vague and endless, as was my conception of the new trail I had taken and my dream of the far-off goal.

My father's farm of 160 acres, which he had taken up and improved under the United States Homestead laws, lay along the north bank of the river. The nearest neighbor lived a mile away, and all had flourishing fields of wheat, Indian corn, and potatoes. Some two miles distant, where the Big Sioux doubled upon itself, rose the mission church and schoolhouse, the only frame building within forty miles.

Our herd of ponies was loose upon the prairie, and it was my first task each morning to bring them into the log corral. On this particular morning I lingered, finding some of them, like myself, who loved their freedom too well and would not come in.

The man who had built the cabin—it was his first house, and therefore he was proud of it—was tall and manly looking. He stood in front of his pioneer home with a resolute face.

He had been accustomed to the buffalo-skin tepee all his life, until he opposed the white man and was defeated and made a prisoner of war at Davenport, Iowa. It was because of his meditation during those four years in a military prison that he had severed himself from his tribe and taken up a homestead. He declared that he would never join in another Indian outbreak but would work with his hands for the rest of his life.

"I have hunted every day," he said, "for the support of my family. I sometimes chase the deer all day. One must work, and work hard, whether chasing the deer or planting corn. After all, the corn-planting is the surer provision."

These were my father's new views, and in this radical change of life, he had persuaded a few other families to join him. They then had formed a little colony at Flandreau, on the Big Sioux River.

To be sure, his beginnings in civilization had not been attended with all the success that he had hoped for. One year, all of the crops had been devoured by grasshoppers, and another year ruined by drought. But he was still satisfied that there was no alternative for the Indian. He was now anxious to have his boys learn the English language and something about books, for he could see that these were the "bow and arrows" of the white man.

"O-hee-ye-sa!" called my father, and I obeyed the call. "It is time for you to go to school, my son," he said, with his usual air of decision. We had spoken of the matter more than once, yet it seemed hard when it came to the actual undertaking.

I remember quite well how I felt as I stood there with eyes fixed upon the ground.

"And what am I to do at the school?" I asked finally, with much embarrassment.

"You will be taught the language of the white man, and also how to count your money and tell the prices of your horses and of your furs. The white teacher will first teach you the signs by which you can make out the words on their books. They call them *A, B, C,* and so forth. Old as I am, I have learned some of them."

The matter having been thus far explained, I was soon on my way to the little mission school, two miles distant over the prairie. There was no clear idea in my mind as to what I had to do, but as I galloped along the road, I turned over and over what my father had said, and the more I thought of it, the less I was satisfied. Finally I said aloud:

"Why do we need a sign language, when we can both hear and talk?" And unconsciously I pulled on the lariat and the pony came to a stop. I suppose I was half curious and half in dread about this "learning white men's ways." Meanwhile the pony had begun to graze.

While thus absorbed in thought, I was suddenly

startled by the yells of two other Indian boys and the noise of their ponies' hoofs. I pulled the pony's head up just as the two strangers also pulled up. They stopped their panting ponies at my side. They stared at me for a minute, while I looked at them out of the corners of my eyes.

"Where are you going? Are you going to our school?" volunteered one of the boys at last.

To this I replied timidly: "My father told me to go to a place where the white men's ways are taught, and to learn the sign language."

"That's good—we are going there, too! Come on, Red Feather, let's try another race! I think, if we had not stopped, my pony would have outrun yours. Will you race with us?" he continued, addressing me, and we all started our ponies at full speed.

I soon saw that the two strange boys were riding erect and soldierlike. "That must be because they have been taught to be like the white man," I thought. I allowed my pony a free start and leaned forward until the animal drew deep breaths; then I slid back and laid my head against the pony's shoulder, at the same time raising my quirt, and he leaped forward with a will! I yelled as I passed the other boys and pulled up when I reached the crossing. The others stopped, too, and surveyed pony and rider from head to foot, as if they had never seen us before.

"You have a fast pony. Did you bring him back with you from Canada?" Red Feather asked. "I think you are the son of Many Lightnings."

"Yes, this is my own pony. My uncle in Canada always used him to chase the buffalo, and he has ridden him in many battles." I spoke with considerable pride.

"Well, as there are no more buffalo to chase now, your pony will have to pull the plow like the rest. But if you ride him to school, you can join the races. On the holy days the young men race horses, too." Red Feather and White Fish spoke both together, while I listened attentively, for everything was strange to me.

"What do you mean by the holy days?" I asked.

"Well, that's another of the white people's customs. Every seventh day they call a holy day, and on that day they go to a Holy House, where they pray to their Great Mystery. They also say that no one should work on that day."

This definition of Sunday and churchgoing set me to thinking again, for I never knew before that there was any difference in the days.

"But how do you count the days, and how do you know what day to begin with?" I inquired.

"Oh, that's easy! The white men have everything in their books. They know how many days in a year, and they have even divided the day itself into so many equal parts; in fact, they have divided them again and again until they know how many times one can breathe in a day," said White Fish, with the air of a learned man.

"That's impossible," I thought, so I shook my head.

By this time we had reached the second crossing of

the river, on whose bank stood the little mission school. Thirty or forty Indian children stood about, curiously watching the newcomer as we came up the steep bank. I realized for the first time that I was an object of curiosity, and it was not a pleasant feeling. On the other hand, I was considerably interested in the strange appearance of these schoolchildren.

They all had on some apology for white man's clothing, but their pantaloons belonged neither to the order *short* nor to the *long*. Their coats, some of them, met only halfway by the help of long strings. Others were lapped over in front and held on by a string of some sort fastened round the body. Some of their hats were brimless and others without crowns, while most were fantastically painted. The hair of all the boys was cut short, and, in spite of the evidences of great effort to keep it down, it stood erect like porcupine quills. I thought, as I stood on one side and took a careful observation of the motley gathering, that if I had to look like these boys in order to obtain something of the white man's learning, it was time for me to rebel.

The boys played ball and various other games, but I tied my pony to a tree and then walked up to the schoolhouse and stood there as still as if I had been glued to the wall. Presently the teacher came out and rang a bell, and all the children went in, but I waited for some time before entering and then slid inside and took the seat nearest the door. I felt singularly out of place, and for the twentieth time wished my father had not sent me.

When the teacher spoke to me, I had not the slightest idea what he meant, so I did not trouble myself to make any demonstration, for fear of giving offense. Finally he asked in broken Sioux: "What is your name?" Evidently he had not been among the Indians long, or he would not have asked that question. It takes a tactician and a diplomat to get an Indian to tell his name! The poor man was compelled to give up the attempt.

He then gave some unintelligible directions, and, to my great surprise, the pupils in turn held their books open and talked the talk of a strange people. Afterward the teacher made some curious signs upon a blackboard on the wall and seemed to ask the children to read them. To me they did not compare in interest with my bird's-track and fish-fin studies on the sands. I was something like a wild cub who was caught overnight, appearing in the corral next morning with the lambs. I had seen nothing thus far to prove to me the good of civilization.

Meanwhile the children grew more familiar, and whispered references were made to the "new boy's" personal appearance. At last he was called "Baby" by one of the big boys; but this was not meant for him to hear, so he did not care to hear. He rose silently and walked out. He did not dare to do or say anything in departing. The boys watched him as he led his pony to the river to drink and then jumped upon his back and started for home at a good pace. They cheered as he started over the hills: "Hoo-oo! hoo-oo! there goes the long-haired boy!"

When I was well out of sight of the school, I pulled in my pony and made him walk slowly home.

"Will going to that place make a man brave and strong?" I asked myself. "I must tell my father that I cannot stay here. I must go back to my uncle in Canada, who taught me to hunt and shoot and to be a brave man. They might as well try to make a buffalo build houses like a beaver as to teach me to be a white man," I thought.

It was growing late when at last I appeared at the cabin. "Why, what is the matter?" quoth my old grandmother, who had taken especial pride in me as a promising young hunter. Really, my face had assumed a look of distress and mental pressure that frightened the superstitious old woman. She held her peace, however, until my father returned.

"Ah," she said then, "I never fully believed in these new manners! The Great Mystery cannot make a mistake. I say it is against our religion to change the customs that have been practiced by our people ages back—so far back that no one can remember it. Many of the schoolchildren have died, you have told me. It is not strange. You have offended Him, because you have made these children change the ways he has given us. I must know more about this matter before I give my consent." Grandmother had opened her mind in unmistakable terms, and the whole family was listening to her in silence.

Then my hard-headed father broke the pause. "Here is one Sioux who will sacrifice everything to win the wisdom of the white man! We have now entered upon this life, and there is no going back. Besides, one would be like a hobbled pony without learning to live like those among whom we must live."

During my father's speech, my eyes had been fixed upon the burning logs that stood on end in the huge mud chimney in a corner of the cabin. I didn't want to go to that place again; but father's logic was too strong for me, and the next morning I had my long hair cut and started in to school in earnest.

I obeyed my father's wishes and went regularly to the little day school, but as yet my mind was in darkness. "What has all this talk of books to do with hunting, or even with planting corn?" I thought. The subject occupied my thoughts more and more, doubtless owing to my father's decided position on the matter; on the other hand, my grandmother's view of this new life was not encouraging.

I took the situation seriously enough, and I remember I went with it where all my people go when they want light—into the thick woods. I needed counsel, and human counsel did not satisfy me. I had been taught to seek the Great Mystery in silence, in the deep forest or on the height of the mountain. I retired into the woods. I knew nothing of the white man's religion; I only followed my ancestors' teaching.

When I came back, my heart was strong. I desired to follow the new trail to the end. I knew that, like the little brook, it must lead to larger and larger ones until it became a resistless river.

"You must not fear to work with your hands," said my father, "but if you are able to think strongly and well, that will be a quiver full of arrows for you, my son. All of the white man's children must go to school, but those who study best and longest need not work with their hands after that, for they can work with their minds. You may plow the five acres next to the river, and see if you can make a straight furrow as well as a straight shot."

I set to work with the heavy breaking plow and yoke of oxen, but I am sorry to admit that the work was poorly done. "It will be better for you to go away to a higher school," advised my father.

It appears remarkable to me now that my father, thorough Indian as he was, should have had such deep and sound conceptions of a true civilization. But there is the contrast—my father's mother!

To her such a life as we lead today would be no less than sacrilege. "It is not a true life," she often said. "It is a sham. I cannot bear to see my boy live a made-up life!" Ah, Grandmother! you had forgotten one of the first principles of your own teaching, namely: "When you see a new trail, or a footprint that you do not know, follow it to the point of knowing."

"I find," said my father to me, "that the white man has a well-grounded religion and teaches his children the same virtues that our people taught to theirs. The Great Mystery has shown to the red and white man alike the good and evil, from which to choose. I think the way of the white man is better than ours because

A log cabin residence at Flandreau, South Dakota

*Dr. Alfred L. Riggs, head of the mission school
at Santee Agency, Nebraska*

From the Deep Woods to Civilization

he is able to preserve on paper the things he does not want to forget. He records everything—the sayings of his wise men, the laws enacted by his counselors."

I began to be really interested in this curious scheme of living that my father was gradually unfolding to me out of his limited experience.

"The way of knowledge," he continued, "is like our old way of hunting. You begin with a mere trail—a footprint. If you follow that faithfully, it may lead you to a clearer trail—a track—a road. Later on there will be many tracks, crossing and diverging one from the other. Then you must be careful, for success lies in the choice of the right road.

"You must be doubly careful, for traps will be laid for you, of which the most dangerous is the spirit-water that causes a man to forget his self-respect," he added, unwittingly giving to his aged mother material for her argument.

The general effect upon me of these discussions, which were logical enough on the whole, although almost entirely from the outside, was that I became convinced that my father was right.

My grandmother had to yield at last, and it was settled that I was to go to school at Santee Agency, Nebraska, where Dr. Alfred L. Riggs was then fairly started in the work of his great mission school, which has turned out some of the best-educated Sioux Indians.[1] It was then the Mecca of the Sioux country, even

---

[1] Under the supervision of Dr. Alfred L. Riggs, the Santee Normal Training School opened in 1870. Considered by many in the

though Sitting Bull and Crazy Horse were still at large, harassing soldiers and emigrants alike, and General Custer had just been placed in military command of the Dakota Territory.[2]

Indian Service as the educational center for all Sioux students, the school offered a core curriculum of religion, arithmetic, geography, music, reading, and writing.

[2]Sitting Bull (Tatanka Iyotake; ca. 1831-90) was the leading chief and holy man of the Hunkpapa Lakota. He strongly opposed Euro-American settlement on the tribal lands. Crazy Horse (Tasunca-uitco; ca. 1842-77), or more accurately "His Horse Is Crazy," was a highly skilled military leader who won several battles against the army. Although Lt. Col. George Armstrong Custer (1839-76) was appointed a general during the Civil War, he was downgraded at its end. He later commanded the newly created Seventh Cavalry, which was transferred to Dakota in 1873. After his 1874 expedition to the Black Hills, he claimed that there was gold in that area. As a result, white miners poured into Sioux territory. A large number of Sioux, Cheyenne, and Arapaho gathered with Sitting Bull near the Rosebud and Little Bighorn Rivers in Montana. On 25 June 1876, Crazy Horse led his mostly Cheyenne force in the attack against Custer, who, along with most of his soldiers, was killed. Although Sitting Bull fled to Canada, Crazy Horse continued to fight against the troops of Gen. Nelson Miles. He finally surrendered on 6 May 1877. On 5 September 1877, he was arrested for leaving the agency without permission. When he resisted, his arms were held by a rival warrior and a soldier bayoneted him.

XV

On the White Man's Trail

IT WAS in the fall of 1874 that I started from Flandreau, then only an Indian settlement, with a good neighbor of ours on his way to Santee. There were only a dozen houses or so at Sioux Falls, and the whole country was practically uninhabited when we embarked in a homemade prairie schooner on that bright September morning.

I had still my Hudson Bay flintlock gun, which I had brought down with me from Canada the year before. I took that old companion, with my shot pouch and a well-filled powder horn. All I had besides was a blanket and an extra shirt. I wore my hunting suit, which was a compromise between Indian attire and a frontiersman's outfit. I was about sixteen years old and small for my age.

"Remember, my boy, it is the same as if I sent you on your first warpath. I shall expect you to conquer," was my father's farewell. My good grandmother, who had brought me up as a motherless child, bestowed upon me her blessing. "Always remember," said she, "that the Great Mystery is good; evil can come only from ourselves!" Thus, I then parted with my first teacher—the woman who taught me to pray!

Our first night out was at Hole-in-the-Hill, one of

the most picturesque spots in the valley. Here I brought in a doe, which I had come upon.

The next morning was frosty, and after an early breakfast we hurried to our traps. I got two fine minks and a beaver for my trouble, while Peter came home smiling with two otters and three beavers. I saw that he had something on his mind, but, like a true Indian, I held my peace. At last he broke the news to me—he had changed his mind about going to Santee Agency!

I did not blame him—it was hard to leave such a trapper's paradise as this, alive with signs of otter, mink, and beaver. I said nothing but thought swiftly. The temptation was strong to remain and trap, too. That would please my grandmother; and I will confess here that no lover is more keen to do the right thing for the loved one than I was at that time to please my old grandmother.

The thought of my father's wish kept me on my true course. Leaving my gun with Peter, I took my blanket and started for the Missouri on foot.

"Tell my father," I said, "that I shall not return until I finish my warpath."

But the voice of the waterfall, near what is now the city of Sioux Falls, sounded like the spirits of woods and water crying for their lost playmate, and I thought for a moment of turning back to Canada, there to regain my freedom and wild life. Still, I had sent word to my father that this warpath should be completed, and I remembered how he had said that if I did not return, he would shed proud tears.

About this time I did some of the hardest thinking that I have ever done in my life. All day I traveled and did not see anyone until, late in the afternoon, descending into the valley of a stream, I came suddenly upon a solitary farmhouse of sod and was met by a white man—a man with hair on his face.

I was hungry and thirsty as a moose in burned timber. I had some money that my father had given me—I hardly knew the different denominations. So I showed the man all of it and told him by signs that he might take what he pleased if only he would let me have something to eat and a little food to carry with me. As for lodging, I would not have slept in his house if he had promised me a war bonnet!

While he was cordial—at any rate, after I exhibited my money—there was something about his manner that did not put me at my ease, and my wild instincts told me to keep an eye on him. But I was not alone in this policy, for his flock of four daughters and a son nearly put their necks out of joint in following my modest, shy movements.

When they invited me to sit down with them at the table, I felt uncomfortable, but hunger was stronger than my fears and modesty. The climax came when I took my seat on a rickety stool between the big, hairy man and one of his well-grown daughters. I felt not unlike a young blue heron just leaving the nest to partake of his first meal on an unsafe, swinging branch. I was entirely uncertain of my perch.

All at once, without warning, the man struck the

table with the butt of his knife with such force that I
jumped and was within an ace of giving a war whoop.
In spite of their taking a firm hold of the homemade
table to keep it steady, the dishes were quivering and
the young ladies no longer able to maintain their composure. Severe glances from mother and father soon
brought us calm, when it appeared that the blow on
the table was merely a signal for quiet before saying
grace. I pulled myself in, much as a turtle would do,
and possibly it should be credited to the stoicism of
my race that I scarcely ever ate a heartier meal.

After supper I got up and held out to the farmer
nearly all the money I had. I did not care whether he
took it all or not. I was grateful for the food, and
money had no such hold on my mind as it has gained
since. To my astonishment, he simply smiled, shook
his head, and stroked his shaggy beard.

I was invited to join the family in the sod-house
parlor, but owing to the severe nerve shocks that I had
experienced at the supper table, I respectfully declined and betook myself to the bank of a stream near
by, where I sat down to meditate. Presently there
pealed forth a peculiar, weird music, and the words of
a strange song. It was music from a melodeon, but I
did not then know what that was; and the tune was
"Nearer My God, to Thee." Strange as it sounded to
me, I felt that there was something soothing and gentle about the music and the voices.

After a while, curiosity led me back to the sod
house, and I saw for the first time how the white

woman pumps so much air into a box that when she presses on the top boards it howls convulsively. I forgot my bashfulness so far as to listen openly and enjoy the operation, wondering much how the white man puts a pair of lungs into a box, which is furnished with a whole set of black and white teeth, and when he sings to it, it appears to answer him.

Presently, I walked over to a shed where the farmer seemed to be very busy with his son, earnestly hammering something with all their might in the midst of glowing fire and sparks. He had an old breaking plow, which he was putting into shape on his rude forge. He had his sleeves rolled up. With his face and hands blackened and his face streaming down with sweat, I thought he looked not unlike a successful warrior just returned from the field of battle. His powerful muscles and the manly way in which he handled the iron impressed me tremendously. "I shall learn that profession if ever I reach the school and learn the white man's way," I thought.

I thanked the good man for his kind invitation to sleep within the sod walls with all his family but signed to him that I preferred to sleep out-of-doors. I could see some distrust in his eyes, for his horses were in the open stable; and at that my temper rose, but I managed to control it. He had been kind to me, and no Indian will break the law of hospitality unless he has lost all the trails of his people. The man looked me over again carefully and appeared satisfied; and I rolled myself up in my blanket among the willows, but every star that night seemed to be bent upon telling the story of the white man.

I slept little, and early the next morning I was awakened by the barking of the farmer's collie and the laughter of his daughters. I got up and came to the house. Breakfast was nearly ready, and every member of the family was on hand. After breakfast I once more offered my money but was refused. I was glad. Then and there I loved civilization and renounced my wild life.

I took up my blanket and continued on my journey, which for three days was a lonely one. I had nothing with which to kill any game, so I stopped now and then at a sod house for food. When I reached the back hills of the Missouri, there lay before me a long slope leading to the river bottom, and upon the broad flat, as far as my eyes could reach, lay farmhouses and farms. Ah! I thought, this is the way of civilization, the basis upon which it rests! I desired to know that life.

Thirty miles from the school I met Dr. Riggs on the road, coming to the town of Yankton, and received some encouraging words from him, for he spoke the Sioux language very well. A little further on I met the Indian agent, Major Sears, a Quaker, and he, too, gave me a word of encouragement when he learned that I had walked 150 miles to school. My older brother John, who was then assistant teacher and studying under Dr. Riggs, met me at the school and introduced me to my new life.

The bell of the old chapel at Santee summoned the

pupils to class. Our principal read aloud from a large book and offered prayer. Although he conducted devotional exercises in the Sioux language, the subject matter was still strange, and the names he used were unintelligible to me. *Jesus* and *Jehovah* fell upon my ears as mere meaningless sounds.

I understood that he was praying to the Great Mystery that the work of the day might be blessed and their labor be fruitful. A cold sweat came out upon me as I heard him ask the Great Mystery to be with us in that day's work in that school building. I thought it was too much to ask of Him. I had been taught that the Supreme Being is only concerned with spirits and that when one wishes to commune with Him in nature, he must be in a spiritual attitude and must retire from human sound or influence, alone in the wilderness. Here for the first time I heard Him addressed openly in the presence of a house full of young men and young girls!

All of the scholars were ordered to various rooms under different instructors, and I was left in the chapel with another young man. He was a Mandan from Fort Berthold—one of our ancient enemies. Not more than two years before that time my uncle had been on the warpath against this tribe and had brought home two Mandan scalps. He, too, was a new scholar, and looked as if he were about to come before the judge to receive his sentence. My heart at once went out to him, although the other pupils were all of my own tribe, the Sioux. I noticed that he had beautiful long hair arranged in two plaits, and in spite of his sad face he was noble looking and appeared to great advantage, I thought, in contrast with the other pupils, whose hair was cut short and wearing garments not becoming to them at all. This boy, Alfred Mandan, became a very good friend of mine.

Dr. Riggs took me in hand and told me the rules of the school and what was expected of us. There was the chapel, which was used as a church every Sunday and as a schoolhouse on weekdays. There was the Dakota Home for the girls' dormitory—a small, square frame building—and for the boys, a long log house some 200 yards from the chapel under the large cottonwood trees.

Dr. Riggs said that I need not study that first day but could fill up the big bag he brought me with straw from the straw pile back of his barn. I carried it over to the log cabin, where the doctor was before me and had provided a bunk or framework for my bed. I filled a smaller bag for a pillow, and, having received the sheets and blankets, I made my first white man's bed under his supervision. When it was done, it looked clean and dignified enough for anyone, I thought.

He said that I must make it every morning like that before going to school. "And for your wash, there is a tin basin or two on a bench just outside of the door, by the water barrels." And so it was. We had three barrels of Missouri River water, which we ourselves filled up every week, for we boys had to furnish our own water and wood, and were detailed in pairs for this work.

Dr. Riggs supplied axes for the woodchoppers and barrels and pails for the water carriers, also a yoke of large and gentle white oxen and a lumber wagon. It seems to me that I never was better acquainted with two animals than with these two! I have done some of my solemnest thinking behind them. The Missouri River was about two miles from our log house, with a wide stretch of bottomland intervening, partly cottonwood timber and partly open meadow with tall grass. I could take a nap, or dance a war dance, if I cared to do so, while they were carrying me to wood or to water.

Dr. Riggs gave me a little English primer to study, also one or two books in the Dakota language, which I had learned to read in the day school.

There was a translation of the Psalms and of the *Pilgrim's Progress.* I must confess that at that time I would have preferred one of grandmother's evening stories, or my uncle's account of his day's experiences in the chase. I thought it was the dullest hunting I had ever known!

Toward evening, a company of three young men arrived from up the river—to all appearance full-fledged warriors. Ah, it was good to see the handsome white, blue, and red blankets worn by these stately Sioux youths! I had not worn one since my return from Canada. My brother got me a suit of clothes and had someone cut my hair, which was already over my ears, as it had not been touched since the year before. I felt like a wild goose with its wings clipped.

Next morning, the day pupils emerged in every direction from the woods and deep ravines where the Indians had made their temporary homes, while we, the log-cabin boarders, came out in Indian file. The chapel bell was tolling as we reached the yard, when my attention was attracted to a pretty lass standing with her parents and Dr. Riggs near the Dakota Home. Then they separated themselves, and the father and mother came toward us, leaving the doctor and the pretty Dakota maiden standing still. All at once the girl began to run toward her parents, screaming pitifully.

"Oh, I cannot, I cannot stay in the white man's house! I'll die, I'll die! Mamma! Mamma!"

The parents stopped and reasoned with the girl, but it was of no use. Then I saw them leading her back to the Dakota Home, in spite of her pleading and begging. The scene made my blood boil, and I suppressed with difficulty a strong desire to go to her aid.

How well I remember the first time we were called upon to recite! In the same primer class were Eagle-Crane, Kite, and their compatriot from up the river. For a whole week we youthful warriors were held up and harassed with words of three letters. Like raspberry bushes in the path, they tore, bled, and sweated us—those little words—*rat*, *cat*, and so forth, until not a semblance of our native dignity and self-respect was left. And we were just the age when the Indian youth is most on his dignity! Imagine the same fellows turned loose against Custer or Harney[1] with anything like equal numbers and weapons, and those tried generals would feel like boys! We had been bred and trained to those things; but when we found ourselves within four walls and set to pick out words of three letters, we were like novices upon snowshoes—often flat on the ground.

I hardly think I was ever tired in my life until those first days of boarding school. All day things seemed to come and pass with a wearisome regularity, like walking railway ties—the step was too short for me. At times I felt something of the fascination of the new life, and again there would arise in me a dogged resistance, and a voice seemed to be saying, "It is cowardly to depart from the old things!"

Aside from repeating and spelling words, we had to count and add imaginary amounts. We never had had any money to count, nor potatoes, nor turnips, nor bricks. Why, we valued nothing except honor; that cannot be purchased! It seemed now that everything must be measured in time or money or distance. And when the teacher placed before us a painted globe and said that our world was like that—that upon such a

[1]From 1855 to 1856, William Selby Harney (1800-89) terrorized the Lakota in the upper Missouri River region. Called "Mad Bear" by the Sioux, Harney earned the nickname "Squaw Killer Harney" for his attack against the Sicangu or Brulé Lakota village of Little Thunder, near Ash Holly, Nebraska. Refusing Little Thunder's attempt to surrender, Harney ordered his men to attack on 3 September 1855. They destroyed the village and killed more than 100 men, women, and children.

thing our forefathers had roamed and hunted for untold ages, as it whirled and danced around the sun in
space—I felt that my foothold was deserting me. All
my savage training and philosophy were in the air, if
these things were true.

Later on, when Dr. Riggs explained to us the in-
dustries of the white man, his thrift and forethought,
we could see the reasonableness of it all. Economy is
the able assistant of labor, and the two together pro-
duce great results. The systems and methods of business were of great interest to us, and especially the
adoption of a medium of exchange.

The doctor's own personality impressed us deeply,
and his words of counsel and daily prayers, strange to
us at first, in time found root in our minds. Next to my
own father, this man did more than perhaps any other
to make it possible for me to grasp the principles of
true civilization. He also strengthened and developed
in me that native strong ambition to win out, by sticking to whatever I might undertake. Associated with
him was another man who influenced me powerfully
toward Christian living. This was the Rev. Dr. John P.
Williamson, the pioneer Presbyterian missionary.[2]
The world seemed gradually to unfold before me, and
the desire to know all that the white man knows was
the tremendous and prevailing thought in me and was
constantly growing upon me more and more.

[2]Like his father, Thomas, Rev. Dr. John Williamson (1825-1917)
was dedicated to helping the Santees.

My father wrote to me in the Dakota language for my encouragement. Dr. Riggs had told him that I was not afraid of books or of work but rather determined to profit by them. "My son," he wrote, "I believe that an Indian can learn all that is in the books of the white man, so that he may be equal to them in the ways of the mind!"

I studied harder than most of the boys. Missionaries were poor, and the government policy of education for the Indian had not been developed. The white man in general had no use for the Indian. Sitting Bull and the Northern Cheyennes were still fighting in Wyoming and Montana,[3] so that the outlook was not bright for me to pursue my studies among the whites, yet it was now my secret dream and ambition.

It was at Santee that I sawed my first cord of wood. Before long I had a little money of my own, for I sawed most of Dr. Riggs's own wood and some at the Dakota

---

[3]Allies of the Sioux, the Northern Cheyenne fought with them at the Battle of the Little Bighorn in 1876. Sitting Bull and his followers then fled to Canada. Faced with starvation, Sitting Bull and his people returned to the United States, where he surrendered in 1881. Many Northern Cheyenne remained allies of Crazy Horse, until the Lakota leader was murdered in 1877. Subsequently, the government sent many of the defeated Northern Cheyenne to the Southern Cheyenne–Arapaho Reservation in Indian Territory (now Oklahoma). Because of the harsh conditions there, 300 Northern Cheyenne escaped and tried to reach Fort Robinson, Nebraska, where they were imprisoned. In January 1879, troops killed thirty Cheyenne as they tried to escape. Four years later, the Northern Cheyenne moved to a reservation on the Tongue River in Montana.

Home, besides other work for which I was paid. Although I could not understand or speak much English, at the end of my second year, I could translate every word of my English studies into the native tongue, besides having read all that was then published in the Sioux. I had caught up with boys who had two or three years the start of me and was now studying elementary algebra and geometry.

One day Dr. Riggs came to me and said that he had a way by which he could send me to Beloit, Wisconsin, to enter the preparatory department of Beloit College.[4] This was a great opportunity, and I grasped it eagerly, though I had not yet lost my old timidity about venturing alone among the white people.

On the eve of departure, I received word from Flandreau that my father was dead, after only two days' illness. He was still in the prime of life and a tireless worker. This was a severe shock to me, but I felt even more strongly that I must carry out his wishes. It was clear that he who had sought me out among the wild tribes at the risk of his life and set my feet in the new trail should be obeyed to the end. I did not go back to my home, but in September 1876, I started from Santee to Beloit to begin my serious studies.

[4]Beloit College, founded in 1846-47, is located in Beloit, Wisconsin, about seventy miles southwest of Milwaukee. One of the founders of the National Education Association, Aaron L. Chapin was president from 1849 to 1885.

XVI

College Life in the West

T HE JOURNEY to Beloit College was an education in itself. At Yankton City I boarded the train for the first time in my life, but not before having made a careful inspection of the locomotive—that fiery monster which had so startled me on my way home from Canada. Every hour brought new discoveries and new thoughts—visions that came and passed like the telegraph poles as we sped by. More and more we seemed to me to be moving upon regions too small for the inhabitants. Towns and villages grew ever larger and nearer together, until at last we reached a city of some little size where it was necessary for me to change cars, a matter that had been arranged by Dr. Riggs with the conductor. The streets looked crowded, and everybody seemed to be in the greatest possible hurry. I was struck with the splendor of the shops and the brilliant show windows. Someone took me to an eating house and left me alone with the pretty waitress, whose bright eyes and fluent speech alarmed me. I thought it best to agree with everything she said, so I assented with a nod of the head, and I fancy she brought me everything that was on the bill of fare!

When I reached Beloit on the second day of my pilgrimage, I found it beautifully located on the high, wooded banks of Black Hawk's[1] picturesque Rock River. The college grounds covered the site of an ancient village of mound builders, which showed to great advantage on the neat campus, where the green grass was evenly cut with lawnmowers. I was taken to President Chapin's house, and after a kindly greeting, shown to my room in South College, where I immediately opened all of the windows. A young man emerged from our building, and I could distinctly hear him shouting to another across the Common:

"Hurry up, Turkey, or you'll not have the chance to face old Petty again! We have Sitting Bull's nephew right here, and it's more than likely he'll have your scalp-lock before morning!"

"Turkey," as I soon learned, was the son of a missionary to that country, and both of these boys became good friends of mine afterward.

It must be remembered that this was September 1876, less than three months after Custer's gallant

[1]During the War of 1812, the leader of the Sac, Black Hawk, (Makataimeshekiakiak; 1767-1838) led hundreds of tribesman to Detroit to fight on the side of the British. By 1831, he was the spokesman for Sac, Mesquakie, and other Indians who refused to migrate west of the Mississippi. In 1832, he led his "British Band" into Illinois to establish farms. Because of public outrage, President Andrew Jackson sent federal troops to pursue the Indians. Abraham Lincoln, who served as captain in the volunteers during 1832, joked that he saw no "live, fighting Indians" during the war but had "a good many bloody struggles with the mosquitoes." Chased into southern Wisconsin, the band was defeated at Bad Axe River. After being imprisoned in Virginia for several months, Black Hawk returned in disgrace to his tribe.

command was annihilated by the hostile Sioux. I was especially troubled when I learned that my two uncles whom we left in Canada had taken part in this famous fight. People were bitter against the Sioux in those days, and I think it was a nephew of Sitting Bull who had sent me there to study the white man's arts so that he might be better able to cope with him. When I went into town, I was followed on the streets by gangs of little white savages, giving imitation war whoops.

My first recitation at Beloit was an event in my life. I was brought before a remarkable-looking man whose name was Professor Pettibone. He had a long, grave face, long whiskers, and scarcely any hair on his head, and was to me the very embodiment of wisdom. I was already well drilled in the elementary studies, except that I was very diffident about speaking the English language and found it hard to recite or to demonstrate mathematical problems. However, I made every effort and soon learned to speak quite fluently, although not correctly; but that fact did not discourage me.

I was now a stranger in a strange country, and deep in a strange life from which I could not retreat. I was like a deaf man with eyes continually on the alert for expressions of faces, and to find them as general friendly toward me was somewhat reassuring. In spite of some nerve-trying moments, I soon recovered my balance and set to work. I absorbed knowledge through every pore. The more I got, the larger my capacity grew, and my appetite increased in proportion. I discovered that my anticipations of this new life were nearly all wrong, and was suddenly confronted with problems entirely foreign to my experience. If I had been told to swim across a lake or run with a message through an unknown country, I should have had some conception of the task; but the idea of each word as having an office and a place and a specific name, and standing in relation to other words like the bricks in a wall, was almost beyond my grasp. As for history and geography, to me they were legends and traditions, and I soon learned to appreciate the pure logic of mathematics. A recent letter from a Beloit schoolmate says, "You were the only boy who could beat me in algebra!"

At Beloit I spent three years of student life. While in some kinds of knowledge I was the infant of the college, in athletics I did my full share. To keep myself at my best physically, I spent no less than three hours daily in physical exercise, and this habit was kept up throughout my college days.

I found among other students many who were self-supporting, either the sons of poor parents, or self-reliant youth who preferred to earn money for at least a part of their expenses. I soon discovered that these young men were usually among the best students. Since I had no means of my own and the United States government had not then formulated the policy of Indian education, I was ready for any kind of work, and on Saturdays I usually sawed wood and did other chores for the professors.

During the first summer vacation, I determined to hire out as a farmer. Armed with a letter of introduction from President Chapin, I set out in a southerly direction. As I walked, I recalled the troubles of that great chief of the Sac and Fox tribe, Black Hawk, who had some dispute with President Lincoln about that very region.

At the first farm I came to, I approached the front door with some misgivings. A young lady asked me to wait, and I fancied I read in her clear blue eyes the thoughts that passed through her mind. In ten minutes or so, the farmer came in from the field and entered his home by another door, apparently taking some precautions against a surprise before coming to me where I waited, hungry and tired, on the doorstep.

"Well, young man, what do you want?" quoth he.

I said, "I am a student at Beloit College, but the college is closed for the summer, and I am looking for work."

"Oho! you cannot work the New Ulm game on me.[2] I don't think you can reproduce the Fort Dearborn massacre[3] on this farm. By the way, what tribe do you belong to?"

"I am Sioux," I replied.

[2] On 19 and 23 August 1862, the Santee attacked this German town, located a few miles below the Lower Sioux Reservation. While the first attack accomplished little, that on the twenty-third was well organized. The reinforced settlers pushed back the Santee, but the town was burned and thirty-four men were killed or wounded.

[3] During the War of 1812, the garrison and settlers fled Fort Dearborn in Chicago. A short distance from the fort, a combined force of 400 Indians, primarily Potawatomi and Ottawa (Odawa), killed twenty-six of the fifty-four regular soldiers, all twelve of the militia, two white women, and twelve white children.

"That settles it. Get off from my farm just as quick as you can! I had a cousin killed by your people only last summer."

I kept on my way until I found another farmer to whom I made haste to present my letter. For him I worked all summer, and as treaties were kept on both sides, there was no occasion for any trouble.

It was here and now that my eyes were opened intelligently to the greatness of Christian civilization, the ideal civilization, as it unfolded itself before my eyes. I saw it as the development of every natural resource, the broad brotherhood of mankind, the blending of all languages, and the gathering of all races under one religious faith. There must be no more warfare within our borders; we must quit the forest trail for the breaking plow, since pastoral life was the next thing for the Indian. I renounced finally my bow and arrows for the spade and pen; I took off my soft moccasins and put on the heavy and clumsy but durable shoes. Every day of my life I put into use every English word that I knew, and for the first time permitted myself to think and act as a white man.

At the end of three years, other Sioux Indians had been sent to Beloit, and I felt that I might progress faster where I was not surrounded by my tribesmen. Dr. Riggs arranged to transfer me to the preparatory department of Knox College,[4] at Galesburg, Illinois, of

[4]From fall 1879 through spring 1881, Eastman attended Knox College, Galesburg, located in central Illinois. Chartered in 1837, Knox first admitted women in 1870.

which he himself was a graduate. Here, again, I was thrown into close contact with the rugged, ambitious sons of western farmers. Among my staunch friends at Knox were S.S. McClure, John S. Phillips of the *American Magazine*, Edgar A. Bancroft of Chicago, now attorney for the International Harvester Company, Judge Merritt Pinckney of Chicago, Representative Rainey, and other men who have become well-known and whose friendship is still retained.[5]

As Knox is a coeducational institution, it was here that I mingled for the first time with the paleface maidens, and as soon as I could shake off my Indian shyness, I found them very winning and companionable. It was through social intercourse with the American college girl that I gained my first conception of the home life and domestic ideals of the white man. I had thoroughly learned the Indian club and dumbbell exercises at Beloit, and here at Knox I taught a class of young ladies to meet a part of my expenses.

[5]Born in Ireland, Samuel Sidney McClure (1857-1938) immigrated to the United States at age nine. Founder of the first profitable literary syndicate, he and John Sanburn Phillips (1861-1949) started in 1884 the monthly *McClure's Magazine*. It became famous for its 1903 exposés of corporate and city-government corruption. After breaking with McClure, Phillips became editor of *American Magazine* (1906-15). Edgar A. Bancroft (1857-1925) was general counsel to the International Harvester Company (1907-20) and wrote several books. In 1905, Merritt Willis Pinckney (1859-1920) became a judge of the Cook County Circuit Court and later served on the juvenile court. A member of Congress from 1903 to 1921 and 1923 to 1935, Henry T. Rainey (1860-1934) became Democratic leader of the House in 1933.

Soon I began to lay definite plans for the future. Happily, I had missed the demoralizing influences of reservation life and had been mainly thrown in with the best class of Christian white people. With all the strength of a clean young manhood, I set my heart upon the completion of a liberal education.

The next question to decide was what should be my special work in life. It appeared that in civilization one must have a definite occupation—a profession. I wished to share with my people whatever I might attain, and I looked about me for a distinct field of usefulness apart from the ministry, which was the first to be adopted by the educated Sioux.

Gradually my choice narrowed down to law and medicine, for both of which I had a strong taste. But, the latter seemed to me to offer a better opportunity of service to my race; therefore, I determined upon the study of medicine long before I entered upon college studies. "Hitch your wagon to a star," says the American philosopher, and this was my star!

XVII

College Life in the East

ONE SUMMER vacation, at my home in Dakota, Dr. Riggs told me the story of Dartmouth College in New Hampshire, and how it was originally founded as a school for Indian youth. The news was timely and good news, and yet I hesitated. I dreaded to cut myself off from my people, and in my heart I knew that if I went, I should not return until I had accomplished my purpose. It was a critical moment in my life, but the decision could be only one way. I taught in the little day school where my first lessons had been learned throughout the fall term, and in January 1882, I set out for the far East, at a period when the government was still at considerable trouble to subdue and settle some of my race upon reservations.

Though a man in years, I had very little practical knowledge of the world, and in my inexperience I was still susceptible to the adventurous and curious side of things rather than to their profounder meanings. Therefore, while somewhat prepared, I was not yet conscious of the seriousness and terrific power of modern civilization.

It was a crisp winter morning when the train pulled into Chicago. I had in mind the Fort Dearborn incident, and it seemed to me that we were being drawn into the deep gulches of the Badlands as we entered the city. I realized vividly at that moment that the day of the Indian had passed forever.

I was met at the station by friends who took me to walk upon some of the main streets. I saw a perfect stream of humanity rushing madly along and noticed with some surprise that the faces of the people were not happy at all. They wore an intensely serious look that to me was appalling.

I was cautioned against trusting strangers and was told that I must look out for pickpockets. Evidently there were some disadvantages connected with this mighty civilization, for we Indians seldom found it necessary to guard our possessions. It seemed to me that the most dignified men on the streets were the policemen, in their long blue coats with brass buttons. They were such a remarkable set of men physically that this of itself was enough to catch my eye.

Soon I was again upon the eastern-bound express, and we had not gone far when a middle-aged man who had thoroughly investigated my appearance both through and over his glasses came to my seat and without apology or introduction began to bombard me with countless questions.

"You are an Indian?" he began.

"Yes," I murmured.

"What is your tribe?"

"Sioux."

"How came you so far away from the tribe? Are you a member of Sitting Bull's band? Are you related to him?" he continued. I was greatly relieved when he released me from his intrusive scrutiny. Among our people, children and old women sometimes betray curiosity as regards a stranger, but no grown man would be guilty of such bad manners as I have often met with when traveling.

After we left Albany, I found myself in a country the like of which, I thought, I would have given much to hunt over before it was stripped of its primeval forests, and while deer and bear roamed over it undisturbed. I looked with delight upon mountains and valleys, and even the little hamlets perched upon the shelves of the high hills. The sight of these rocky farms and little villages reminded me of the presence of an earnest and persistent people. Even the deserted farmhouse, the ruined mill, had an air of saying, "I have done my part in the progress of civilization. Now I can rest." And all the mountains seemed to say, Amen.

What is the great difference between these people and my own? I asked myself. Is it not that the one keeps the old things and continually adds to them new improvements, while the other is too well contented with the old and will not change his ways nor seek to improve them?

When I reached Boston, I was struck with the old, mossy, granite edifices, and the narrow, crooked streets. Here, too, the people hurried along as if the gray wolf were on their trail. Their ways impressed me as cold, but I forgot that when I learned to know some of them better.

I went on to Dartmouth College, away up among the granite hills. The country around it is rugged and wild; and thinking of the time when red men lived there in plenty and freedom, it seemed as if I had been destined to come view their graves and bones. No, I said to myself, I have come to continue that which is their last struggle they proposed to take up, in order to save themselves from extinction; but alas! it was too late. Had our New England tribes but followed the example of that great Indian Samson Occum[1] and kept up with the development of Dartmouth College, they would have brought forth leaders and men of culture. This was my ambition—that the Sioux should accept civilization before it was too late! I wished that our young men might at once take up the white man's way, and prepare themselves to hold office and wield influence in their native states. Although this hope has not been fully realized, I have the satisfaction of knowing that not a few Indians now hold positions of trust and exercise some political power.

At Dartmouth College I found the buildings much older and more imposing than any I had seen before.

---

[1] A Mohegan missionary, teacher, and author, Samson Occom or Occum (1723-92) spent two years in England raising more than 12,000 pounds for Moor's Indian Charity School. Supervised by Eleazar Wheelock, the Charity School became Dartmouth College. Occom broke with Wheelock in 1773 after the latter shifted the school's focus from recruiting Native American students to training white missionaries. Subsequently, Occom became the leader of the Christian Brothertown Indians and removed with them to the Oneida nation in central New York.

There was a true scholastic air about them; in fact, the whole village impressed me as touched with the spirit of learning and refinement. My understanding of English was now so much enlarged as to enable me to grasp current events, as well as the principles of civilization, in a more intelligent manner.

At Kimball Union Academy,[2] the little ancient institution at which I completed my preparation for college by direction of President Bartlett of Dartmouth,[3] I absorbed much knowledge of the New Englander and his peculiarities. I found Yankees of the uneducated class very Indian-like in their views and habits; a people of strong character, plain-spoken, and opinionated. However, I observed that the students of the academy and their parents were very frugal and saving. Nothing could have been more instructive to me, as we Indians are inclined to be improvident. I had been accustomed to broad, fertile prairies and liberal ways. Here they seemed to count their barrels of potatoes and apples before they were grown. Every little brooklet was forced to do a river's work in their mills and factories.

I was graduated here and went to old Dartmouth in the fall of 1883 to enter the freshman class. Although

[2]Eastman attended Kimball Union Academy, Meriden, New Hampshire, for a year and a half. It was one of the preparatory schools that students attended before entering Dartmouth.
[3]Samuel Colcord Bartlett (b. 1817) became president of Dartmouth in 1877. Dartmouth College, located in Hanover, New Hampshire, opened in 1770 as a men's school. It is now coeducational.

I had associated with college students for several years, yet I must confess that western college life is quiet compared with that of the tumultuous East. It was here that I had most of my savage gentleness and native refinement knocked out of me. I do not complain, for I know that I had gained more than their equivalent.

On the evening of our first class meeting, lo! I was appointed football captain for my class. My supporters orated quite effectively on my qualifications as a frontier warrior, and some went so far as to predict that I would, when warmed up, scare all the sophs off the premises! These representations seemed to be confirmed when, that same evening after supper, the two classes met in a first "rush," and as I was not acquainted with the men, I held up the professor of philosophy, mistaking him for one of the sophomores. Reporters for the Boston dailies made the most of their opportunity to enlarge upon this incident.

I was a sort of prodigal son of old Dartmouth, and nothing would have exceeded the heartiness of my welcome. The New England Indians, for whom it was founded, had departed well-nigh a century earlier, and now a warlike Sioux, like a wild fox, had found his way into this splendid seat of learning! Though poor, I was really better off than many of the students, since the old college took care of me under its ancient charter. I was treated with the greatest kindness by the president and faculty, and often encouraged to ask questions and express my own ideas. My uncle's observations in natural history, for which he had a positive genius, the Indian standpoint in sociology and political economy, these were the subjects of some protracted discussions in the classroom. This became so well understood that some of my classmates who had failed to prepare their recitations would induce me to take up the time by advancing a native theory of firsthand observation.

For the first time, I became really interested in literature and history. Here it was that civilization began to loom up before me colossal in its greatness, when the fact dawned upon me that nations and tongues, as well as individuals, have lived and died. There were two men of the past who were much in my thoughts: my countryman Occum, who matriculated there a century before me, and the great Daniel Webster (said to have a strain of Indian blood),[4] who came to Dartmouth as impecunious as I was. It was under the Old Pine Tree[5] that the Indians were supposed to have

[4]Daniel Webster (1782-1852), statesman, senator, and orator, came from a New England farm family but was not of American Indian descent.

[5]The area around Dartmouth originally contained many pine trees. One surviving tree, possibly planted in the mid- to late-eighteenth century, was called the Old Pine. Eastman refers to the legend that before three Indians graduated from Dartmouth, they met beneath their favorite pine tree. They vowed to meet again at the spot where they had built a wigwam and had sung to cement their friendship. The song "The Three Indians" or "When Shall We Three Meet Again" grew out of this legend. When the song was published as a broadside around 1812, a note stated that three Indians composed the first part, which they sang at their last meeting. After being struck by lightning in 1887 and suffering wind

met for the last time to smoke the pipe of peace, and under its shadow every graduating class of my day smoked a parting pipe.

I was anxious to help myself as much as possible and gain practical experience at the same time, by working during the long summer vacations. One summer I worked in a hotel; at another time I canvassed for a book, I think it was *Knights of Labor*, published in Boston. Such success as I attained was due less to any business sagacity than to a certain curiosity I seemed to excite and which often resulted in the purchase of the book, whether the subscriber really cared for it or not. Another summer, an old school friend, an Armenian, conceived the scheme of dressing me in native costume and sending me out to sell his goods. When I wore a jacket and fez, and was well scented with attar of rose, no dog would permit me on his master's premises if he could help it. Nevertheless, I did very well. For business purposes I was a Turk, but I never answered any direct questions on the subject of my nativity.

Throughout my student days in the West, I had learned to reverence New England, and especially its metropolis, as the home of culture and art, of morality and Christianity. At that period that sort of thing got a lodging place in my savage mind more readily

---

damage in 1892, Old Pine was cut down in 1895. The preserved stump was adorned with a plaque honoring its significance to the college.

Dartmouth College athletes (Eastman is at upper left)

Courtesy Dartmouth College Library

183

Charles Eastman, 1887

than the idea of wealth or material power. Somehow I had supposed that Boston must be the home of the nation's elect and not far from the millennium. I was very happy when, after my graduation with the class of 1887, it was made possible for me to study medicine at Boston University. The friends who generously assisted me to realize my great ambition were of the type I had dreamed of, and my home influences in their family all that I could have wished for. A high ideal of duty was placed before me, and I was doubly armed in my original purpose to make my education of service to my race. I continued to study the Christ philosophy and loved it for its essential truths, though doctrines and dogmas often puzzled and repelled me. I attended the Shawmut Congregational Church, of which the Reverend William Eliot Griffis[6] was then pastor, and I am happy to say he became my lifelong friend.

Mr. and Mrs. Frank Wood,[7] who were a father and mother to me at this period, were very considerate of

---

[6]Griffis was an educator, clergyman, and author of many books on Japan and on history. From 1870-74, he helped the Japanese government organize schools on the American plan, supervised the establishment of the first technical school in Japan, and was a professor of physics at the Imperial University of Tokyo. An 1877 graduate of Union Theological Seminary, Griffis was pastor of Shawmut Congregational Church, in Boston, Massachusetts, from 1886 to 1893.

[7]The Woods were friends and associates of Thomas Riggs. Frank Wood, a printer, was active in the Lake Mohonk Conference of Friends of the Indian, the Indian Rights Association, and the Boston Indian Citizenship Committee. These organizations dealt with issues of federal Indian policy reform and assimilation.

my health and gave me opportunity to enter into many outdoor sports, such as tennis and canoeing, beside regular gymnasium work. The unique features of old Boston, the park system with the public flower gardens and the Arboretum, the reservoirs, and, above all, the harbor with its vast assemblage of vessels, each of these was a school in itself.

I did much general reading and did not neglect my social opportunities. At Dartmouth I had met the English man of letters, Matthew Arnold, and he was kind enough to talk with me for some time. I have also talked with Emerson, Longfellow, Francis Parkman, and many other men of note.[8] Mr. and Mrs. Wood were trustees of Wellesley College, and I was so fortunate as to be an occasional visitor there and to make the acquaintance of Miss Freeman,[9] its first president. I believe the first lecture I ever delivered in public was before the Wellesley girls. I little dreamed that a daughter of mine would ever be among them![10]

During the three years that I studied in Boston, I went every summer to Mr. Moody's famous summer school at Northfield[11] and was much interested in his

[8]Matthew Arnold (1822-88), English poet, critic, and essayist. Ralph Waldo Emerson (1803-82), American philosopher, essayist, and poet. Henry Wadsworth Longfellow (1807-82), American poet. Francis Parkman (1823-93), American historian.

[9]In 1882, Alice E. Freeman (1855-1902) became the second, not the first, president of Wellesley College, resigning in 1887 to marry Professor George Herbert Palmer of Harvard.

[10]Eastman's daughter, Virginia Eastman, graduated from Wellesley in 1918.

[11]An internationally renowned evangelist, Dwight L. Moody

strong personality. One morning as we walked together, we came to a stone at the roadside. "Eastman," said he, "this stone is a reminder of the cruelty of your countrymen two centuries ago. Here they murdered an innocent Christian."

"Mr. Moody," I replied, "it might have been better if they had killed them all. Then you would not have had to work so hard to save the souls of their descendants."

At the date of my graduation, in 1890, the government had fully committed itself to the new and permanent plan of the education of the young Indians preparatory to admitting them to citizenship. Various philanthropic societies had been formed expressly to help toward this end. These facts gave weight and momentum to my desire to use all that I had learned for their benefit. I soon received my appointment to the position of government physician at the Pine Ridge Agency[12] in South Dakota, to report on 1 October. Meantime, I stayed in Boston and kept books for Mr.

(1837-99), established in 1863 a nondenominational church in Chicago. Concerned about the religious needs of young people from his hometown of Northfield, Massachusetts, he founded the Northfield Seminary for girls in 1879 and the Mount Hermon School for boys in 1881. At Northfield Seminary, he inaugurated in 1880 the first of several summer conferences for Christian workers.

[12]Pine Ridge Indian Agency: Under the Dawes Act of 1887, the Great Sioux Reservation was divided into smaller ones. The Oglala Lakota were settled on the Pine Ridge Reservation. Located in South Dakota near the border of Nebraska, it is the largest of the Lakota reservations.

Wood while his bookkeeper took a vacation, and later secured an extension of time in order to attend the Lake Mohonk Indian Conference.[13] Here I met Mr. Herbert Welsh and Professor Painter of the Indian Rights Association, Bishop Hare, Bishop Whipple, and many others, and listened with great interest to their discussions.[14] I became convinced that the Indians had some real friends, and this gave me much encouragement.

[13]Lake Mohonk Indian Conference: In 1883, the Friends of the Indian held their first weekend conference at Lake Mohonk, New York. The conferences, to which only Protestants were invited, provided a forum where religious leaders, politicians, and reformers heard reports and legislation as well as discussed and debated Indian issues.

[14]Welsh (1851-1941) was a supporter of assimilation through education and allotting tribal land to individual tribal members. In 1882, he founded the Indian Rights Association, which investigated and publicized reservation conditions. Charles C. Painter (d. 1895), a Congregational minister who had been on the faculty of Fisk College, began work with the Indian Rights Association in 1883 and became an accomplished lobbyist and meticulous investigator of conditions on reservations. William Hobart Hare (1838-1909), bishop of the Protestant Episcopal Church, was called the "Apostle to the Sioux." Consecrated as a bishop in 1873, Hare then served the South Dakota Sioux for thirty-seven years. Hare, who strongly influenced Welsh, established many schools and missions in Sioux territory. Henry Benjamin Whipple (1822-1901), Episcopal bishop of Minnesota, established missions among the Ojibwa and the Sioux. A staunch defender of Native people, he tended the Santee after the 1862 Uprising and went to Washington to appeal personally to President Lincoln on behalf of the condemned Dakotas.

XVIII

A Doctor Among the Indians

THE PINE RIDGE Indian Agency was a bleak and desolate-looking place in those days, more especially in a November dust storm such as that in which I arrived from Boston to take charge of the medical work of the reservation. In 1890, a "white doctor" who was also an Indian was something of a novelty, and I was afterward informed that there were many and diverse speculations abroad as to my success or failure in this new role, but at the time I was unconscious of an audience. I was thirty-two years of age, but appeared much younger, athletic, and vigorous, and alive with energy and enthusiasm.

After reporting to the Indian agent, I was shown to my quarters, which consisted of a bedroom, sitting room, office, and dispensary, all in one continuous barrack with the police quarters and the agent's offices. This barrack was a flimsy one-story affair built of warped cottonwood lumber, and the rude prairie winds whistled musically through the cracks. There was no carpet, no furniture save a plain desk and a couple of hard wooden chairs, and everything was coated with a quarter of an inch or so of fine Dakota dust. This did not disconcert me, however, as I myself was originally Dakota dust! An old-fashioned box stove was the only cheerful thing on the premises, and the first duty I performed was to myself. I built a roaring fire in the stove and sat down for a few minutes to take a sort of inventory of the situation and my professional prospects.

I had not yet thought seriously of making a life contract with any young woman, and accordingly my place was at the agency mess where the unmarried employees took their meals. I recall that the cook at that time was a German, and the insistent sauerkraut and other German dishes were new to me and not especially appetizing.

After supper, as I sat alone in my dismal quarters fighting the first pangs of homesickness, an Indian softly opened the door and stepped in without knocking, in characteristic Indian fashion. My first caller was old Blue Horse,[1] chief emeritus of the Loafer band, of which American Horse[2] was the active chief. After greeting me in Sioux, he promptly produced his credentials, which consisted of well-worn papers that had been given him by various high military officers, from General Harney to General Crook,[3] and were

[1]Blue Horse was a chief of the Loafers or Waglukhe. At one time they were a large and important band of the Lakota, but they became increasingly isolated. Blue Horse remained among them.

[2]American Horse (d. 1902), headman of the True-Oglala Lakota band and son-in-law of Red Cloud. After 1868, American Horse settled on the Red Cloud Agency and became a factional leader in the various reservation affairs. In 1889, American Horse helped the government fraudulently deprive the Sioux of half their remaining lands.

[3]In 1875, Gen. George Crook (1828-90), whom the Sioux called "Three Stars," was ordered to clear the Black Hills of some

dated 1854 to 1877. Blue Horse had been, as he claimed, a friend to the white man, for he was one of the first Sioux army scouts and also one of the first to cross the ocean with Buffalo Bill.[4] The old man wanted nothing so much as an audience, and the tale of his exploits served to pass the evening. Someone had brought in a cot and an armful of blankets, and I was soon asleep.

Next morning I hunted up an Indian woman to assist in a general cleaning and overhauling of the premises. My first official act was to close up the "hole in the wall," like a ticket-seller's window, through which my predecessors had been wont to deal out pills and potions to a crowd of patients standing in line. I put a sign outside of the door, which told them to come in.

It so happened that this was the day of the Big Issue, on which thousands of Indians scattered over a reservation a hundred miles long by fifty miles wide came to the agency for a weekly or fortnightly supply of rations. It was a veritable "Wild West" array that greeted my astonished eyes. The streets and stores were alive with a motley crowd in picturesque garb, for all wore their best on these occasions. Every road

---

trespassing prospectors. The next year, Crook led expeditions against the Sioux and Cheyenne, only to be defeated on 17 June at the battle of Rosebud Creek, near present-day Kirby, Montana.

[4]William F. Cody (1846-1917), known as Buffalo Bill, recruited most of the performers in his Wild West Shows from Pine Ridge. The shows began in 1883.

leading to the agency was filled with white-topped lumber wagons, with here and there a more primitive travois, and young men and women on ponies' backs were gaily curvetting over the hills. The Sioux belle of that period was arrayed in grass-green or bright purple calico, loaded down with beads and bangles, and sat astride a spotted pony, holding over her glossy uncovered braids and vermilion-tinted cheeks a gaily colored silk parasol.

Toward noon, the whole population moved out two or three miles to a large corral in the midst of a broad prairie, where a herd of beef cattle was held in readiness by the agency cowboys. An Indian with a stentorian voice, mounted on a post, announced the names of the group whose steer was to be turned loose. Next moment the flying animal was pursued by two or three swift riders with rifles across their saddles. As the cattle were turned out in quick succession, we soon had a good imitation of the old-time buffalo hunt. The galloping, long-horned steers were chased madly in every direction, amid yells and whoops, the firing of guns and clouds of yellow dust, with here and there a puff of smoke and a dull report as one stumbled and fell off.

The excitement was soon over, and men of each group were busy skinning the animals, dressing the meat, and dividing it among the families interested. Meanwhile the older women, with sacks in hand, approached the commissary, where they received their regular dole of flour, bacon, coffee, and sugar. Fires

Beef cattle being issued at Pine Ridge, ca. 1891

Courtesy Minnesota Historical Society

Women wait for government rations at Pine Ridge Agency, 1891

were soon blazing merrily in the various temporary camps scattered over the prairie and in the creek bottoms, and after dinner, horse races and dancing were features of the day. Many white sightseers from adjoining towns were usually on hand. Before night, most of the people had set off in a cloud of dust for their distant homes.

It is no wonder that I was kept on my feet giving out medicine throughout that day, as if from a lemonade stand at a fair. It was evident that many were merely seeking an excuse to have a look at the "Indian white doctor." Most of them diagnosed their own cases and called for some particular drug or ointment; a mixture of cod liver oil and alcohol was a favorite. It surprised them that I insisted upon examining each patient and questioning him in plain Sioux—no interpreter needed! I made a record of the interesting cases and took note of the place where they were encamped, planning to visit as many as possible in their tepees before they took again to the road.

The children of the large government boarding school were allowed to visit their parents on issue day, and when the parting moment came, there were some pathetic scenes. It was one of my routine duties to give written excuses from school when necessary on the ground of illness, and these excuses were in much demand from lonely mothers and homesick little ones. As a last resort, the mother herself would sometimes plead illness and the need of her boy or girl for a few days at home. I was wholly in sympathy with the policy of education for the Indian children, yet by no means hardened to the exhibition of natural feeling. I would argue the matter with the parents as tactfully as I could; but if nothing else would win the coveted paper, the grandmother was apt to be pressed into the service, and her verbal ammunition seemed inexhaustible.

Captain Sword,[5] the dignified and intelligent head of the Indian police force, was very friendly and soon found time to give me a great deal of information about the place and the people. He said finally:

"Kola (my friend), the people are very glad that you have come. You have begun well; we Indians are all your friends. But I fear that we are going to have trouble. I must tell you that a new religion has been proclaimed by some Indians in the Rocky Mountain region, and some time ago, Sitting Bull sent several of his men to investigate.[6] We hear that they have come

[5]An Oglala Lakota, Capt. George Sword (Miwakan; ca. 1847-1910) was the first captain of the U.S. Indian Police among the Oglalas. He was a member of several delegations to Washington and other cities to negotiate with the government. Sword provided Dr. John Walker, who succeeded Charles Eastman as doctor at Pine Ridge, with much valuable information about Oglala life and culture.

[6]Eastman refers to the Ghost Dance, which Wovoka, or Jack Wilson (Paiute; ca. 1858-1932), founded in 1889. According to Wovoka's vision, the Supreme Being instructed him to tell his people to love one another, live in peace, and devote themselves to work. If they followed these directions and danced a ceremony the Supreme Being taught him, they would be united with the dead, death would cease, and whites would disappear forever. Wovoka also preached that if the dancers wore "ghost shirts," whites' gun

Capt. George Sword, Oglala Lakota and head of the Indian police force at Pine Ridge Agency

Sioux Indians dancing in front of Eastman's medical office at Pine Ridge, ca. 1890

Wovoka (Jack Wilson),
the Paiute prophet of the Ghost Dance

Ghost Dancers, ca. 1800

back, saying that they saw the prophet, or Messiah, who told them that he is God's Son whom He had sent into the world a second time. He told them that He had waited nearly 2,000 years for the white men to carry out His teachings, but instead they had destroyed helpless small nations to satisfy their own selfish greed. Therefore He had come again, this time as a Savior to the red people. If they would follow His instructions exactly, in a little while He would cause the earth to shake and destroy all the cities of the white man, when famine and pestilence would come to finish the work. The Indians must live entirely by themselves in their tepees so that the earthquake would not harm them. They must fast and pray and keep up a holy or spirit dance that He taught them. He also ordered them to give up the white man's clothing and make shirts and dresses in the old style.

"My friend," Sword went on, "our reservation has been free from this new teaching until the last few weeks. Quite lately this Ghost Dance was introduced by Slow Bull and Kicking Bear[7] from Rosebud"—a neighboring agency. "It has been rapidly gaining converts in many of the camps. This is what the council today was about. The agent says that the Great Father

---

powder could not harm them. The movement was very influential among the Lakota.

[7] A Miniconjou from Cheyenne River, Kicking Bear was one of the most forceful proponents of the Ghost Dance.

at Washington wants it stopped. I fear the people will not stop. I fear trouble."

I listened in silence, for I was taken entirely by surprise. Shortly afterward, the agent himself, a new man and a political appointee, approached me on the same matter. "I tell you, Doctor," he began, after an exchange of greetings, "I am mighty glad you came here just at this time. We have a most difficult situation to handle, but those men down in Washington don't seem to realize the facts. If I had my way, I would have had troops here before this," he declared with emphasis. "This Ghost Dance craze is the worst thing that has ever taken hold on the Indian race. It is going like wildfire among the tribes, and right here and now the people are beginning to defy my authority, and my Indian police seem to be powerless. I expect every employee on the agency to do his or her best to avert an outbreak." I assured him that he might count on me. "I shall talk to you more fully on the subject as soon as you are settled," he concluded.

I began to think the situation must be serious and decided to consult some of the educated and Christian Indians. At this juncture a policeman appeared with a note and handed me my orders, as I supposed. But when I opened it, I read a gracefully worded welcome and invitation to a tea party at the rectory, "to celebrate," the writer said, "my birthday, and your coming to Pine Ridge." I was caught up by the wind of destiny, but at the moment my only thought was of pleasure in the prospect of soon meeting the Reverend

Indian leaders: Kicking Bear, Young Man Afraid of His Horses, and Standing Bear, ca. 1890

The government's Indian scouts in formation at Pine Ridge Agency, 1891

Charles Smith Cook,[8] the Episcopal missionary. He was a Yankton Sioux, a graduate of Trinity College and Seabury Divinity School, and I felt sure that I should find in him a congenial friend.

I looked forward to the evening with a peculiar interest. Mr. Cook was delightful, and so was his gracious young wife, who had been a New York girl. She had a sweet voice and was a trained musician. They had a little boy three or fours years old. Then I met several young ladies, teachers in the boarding school, and a young man or two, and finally Miss Elaine Goodale,[9] who was not entirely a stranger, as I had read her *Apple Blossoms* in Boston, and some of her later articles on Indian education in the *Independent* and elsewhere. Miss Goodale was supervisor of Indian schools in the Dakotas and Nebraska, and she was then at Pine Ridge on a tour of inspection. She was young for such a responsible position but appeared equal to it in mentality and experience. I thought her very dignified and reserved, but this first evening's acquaintance showed me that she was in

[8]Reverend Charles Smith Cook, Episcopal missionary, graduated from Trinity College in 1881. After studying theology at Seabury Divinity School in Minneapolis, he became a minister and teacher at Pine Ridge, where he died in 1892.

[9]Stationed at the Pine Ridge Agency, Elaine Goodale (1863-1953) became in 1890 the superintendent of all the Indian schools in the two Dakotas. She was born at Sky Farm, her family's country home near South Egremont, Massachusetts. As a young woman, Goodale published two books of poems: *Apple Blossoms: Verses of Two Children* (1878), written with her sister, and *In Berkshire with the Wild Flowers* (1879).

earnest thoroughly and absolutely sincere in her work for the Indians. I might as well admit that her personality impressed me deeply. I had laid my plans carefully and purposed to serve my race for a few years in my profession, after which I would go to some city to practice, and I had decided that it would be wise not to think of marriage for the present. I had not given due weight to the possibility of love.

Events now crowded fast upon one another. It would seem enough that I had at last realized the dream of my life—to be of some service to my people—an ambition implanted by my earlier Indian teachers and fostered by my missionary training. I was really happy in devoting myself mind and body to my hundreds of patients who left me but few leisure moments. I soon found it absolutely necessary to have some help in the dispensary, and I enlisted the aid of George Graham, a Scottish half-breed, and a simple, friendly fellow. I soon taught him to put up the common salves and ointments, the cough syrups and other mixtures that were in most frequent demand. Together we scoured the shelves from top to bottom and prepared as best we could for the issue-day crowds.

After the second Big Issue, I had another call from Captain Sword. He began, I believe, by complimenting me upon a very busy day. "Your reputation," he declared, "has already traveled the length and breadth of the reservation. You treat everybody alike, and your directions are understood by the people. No government doctor has ever gone freely among them before.

It is a new order of things. But I fear you have come at a bad time," he added seriously. "The Ghost Dancers have not heeded the agent's advice and warning. They pay no attention to us policemen. The craze is spreading like a prairie fire, and the chiefs who are encouraging it do not even come to the agency. They send after their rations and remain at home. It looks bad."

"Do they really mean mischief?" I asked incredulously, for Mr. Cook and I had discussed the matter and agreed in thinking that if the attempt was not made to stop it by force, the craze would die out by itself before long.

"They say not, and that all they ask is to be let alone. They say the white man is not disturbed when he goes to church," Sword replied. "I must tell you, however, that the agent has just ordered the police to call in all government employees with their families to the agency. This means something is going to happen. I have heard he will send for soldiers to come here to stop the dance. If so, there will be trouble."

As I was still too new to the situation to grasp it fully, I concluded that in any case the only thing for me to do was to apply myself diligently to my special work and await the issue. I had arranged to give a course of simple talks on physiology and hygiene at the government boarding school. On the evening of my first talk, I came back to my quarters rather late, for I had been invited to join the teachers afterward in their reading circle.

I had given up two of my rooms to Colonel Lee, the

census taker, and his wife, who could find no other shelter in the crowded state of the agency, and found them awaiting me.

"Well, Doc," said the jolly colonel, "I suppose you have fixed your eye on the prettiest of the school teachers by this time!"

"I should be a callous man if I hadn't," I laughed.

"That's the right spirit. And now, here's a big bundle the stage left for you. Open it up, Doc."

The parcel contained a riding suit of corduroy lined with leather, and reversible, also a pair of laced riding boots reaching to the thigh, a present from an old friend in Boston. Nothing could have been more timely, for I now spent a good part of my days and not a few nights in the saddle. I was called to the most distant parts of the reservation and had bought a fine white horse, part Arabian, which I named Jack Frost. When I called for George to saddle him the next morning, I was surprised to have him hesitate.

"Don't you think, Doctor, you had better keep pretty close to the agency until things are a little more settled?" he asked.

"Why, George, what do you mean?"

"Well, this news that the troops have been sent for, whether it is true or not, is making a good deal of talk. No telling what some fool Indian may take it into his head to do next. Some of the white employees are not stopping at the agency; they are going right on to the railroad. I heard one man say there is going to be an Indian outbreak and he intends to get out while he can."

XIX

The Ghost Dance War

A RELIGIOUS CRAZE such as that of 1890-91 was a thing foreign to the Indian philosophy. I recalled that a hundred years before, on the overthrow of the Algonquin nations, a somewhat similar faith was evolved by the astute Delaware prophet, brother to Tecumseh.[1] It meant that the last hope of race entity had departed, and my people were groping blindly after spiritual relief in their bewilderment and misery. I believe that the first prophets of the "Red Christ" were innocent enough and that the people generally were sincere, but there were doubtless some who went into it for self-advertisement and who introduced new and fantastic features to attract the crowd.

[1]Tenskwatawa (ca. 1775- ca. 1837) was the brother of Tecumseh (ca. 1768-1813), a war chief. Both were Shawnee, not Delaware. After falling into a trance in 1805, Tenskwatawa, known as the Prophet, preached that in his vision he learned that the Creator made Native Americans, while The Great Serpent, the source of evil, made white men. He urged the Shawnee and other Indians to minimize their contact with white men and their goods. If the Indians followed his doctrines, their relatives would come back to life and the game would return. The religion spread among the Shawnee and neighboring tribes. In 1809, Tecumseh converted the religious movement into a political alliance. For the next three years, he traveled across Ohio, Michigan, Indiana, and Illinois persuading young warriors to join his alliance.

The Ghost Dancers had gradually concentrated on the Medicine Root Creek and the edge of the Badlands, and they were still further isolated by a new order from the agent, calling in all those who had not adhered to the new religion. Several thousand of these "friendlies" were soon encamped on the White Clay Creek, close by the agency. It was near the middle of December, with weather unusually mild for that season. The dancers held that there would be no snow so long as their rites continued.

An Indian called Little[2] had been guilty of some minor offense on the reservation and had hitherto evaded arrest. Suddenly he appeared at the agency on an Issue day, for the express purpose, as it seemed, of defying the authorities. The assembly room of the Indian police, used also as a council room, opened out of my dispensary, and on this particular morning a council was in progress. I heard some loud talking but was too busy to pay particular attention, though my assistant had gone in to listen to the speeches. Suddenly the place was in an uproar, and George burst into the inner office, crying excitedly "Look out for yourself, friend! They are going to fight!"

I went around to see what was going on. A crowd had gathered just outside the council room, and the police were surrounded by wild Indians with guns and drawn knives in their hands. "Hurry up with

[2]After his arrest for killing cattle, Little was taken to Pine Ridge. Although his friends subsequently rescued him, Little later returned to the reservation.

*American Horse, leader of the
Oglala Lakota, ca. 1880*

*Red Cloud (Mahpiya-Luta), war leader and headman
of the Oglala Lakota during the 1860s, ca. 1880*

Jack Red Cloud, son of Red Cloud,
who criticized American Horse at Pine Ridge

Big Foot's band at the Cheyenne River Agency, August 1890,
five months before they were annihilated at Wounded Knee

them!" one shouted, while another held his stone war club over a policeman's head. The attempt to arrest Little had met with a stubborn resistance.

At this critical moment, a fine-looking Indian in citizen's clothes faced the excited throng and spoke in a clear, steady, almost sarcastic voice.

"Stop! Think! What are you going to do? Kill these men of our own race? Then what? Kill all these helpless white men, women, and children? And what then? What will these brave words, brave deeds lead to in the end? How long can you hold out? Your country is surrounded with a network of railroads; thousands of white soldiers will be here within three days. What ammunition have you? What provisions? What will become of your families? Think, think, my brothers! This is a child's madness."

It was the "friendly" chief, American Horse, and it seems to me as I recall the incident that this man's voice had almost magic power. It is likely that he saved us all from massacre, for the murder of the police, who represented the authority of the government, would surely have been followed by a general massacre. It is a fact that those Indians who upheld the agent were in quite as much danger from their wilder brethren as were the whites; indeed, it was said that the feeling against them was even stronger. Jack Red Cloud,[3] son

[3]Eventually a progressive, Jack Red Cloud was Red Cloud's only son. "Progressive" was the term applied to Indians who cooperated with government policies and the Indian agents. Many did so because they believed this was the only way their people

of the chief, thrust into the face of American Horse. "It is you and your kind," he shouted, "who have brought us to this pass!" That brave man never flinched. Ignoring his rash accuser, he quietly reentered the office; the door closed behind him; the mob dispersed and for the moment the danger seemed over.

That evening I was surprised by a late call from American Horse, the hero of the day. His wife entered close behind him. Scarcely were they seated when my door again opened softly, and Captain Sword came in, followed by Lieutenant Thunder Bear and most of the Indian police. My little room was crowded. I handed them some tobacco, which I had always at hand for my guests, although I did not smoke myself. After a silence, the chief got up and shook hands with me ceremoniously. In a short speech, he asked my advice in the difficult situation that confronted them between the Ghost Dancers, men of their own blood, and the government to which they pledged their loyalty.

Thanks to Indian etiquette, I could allow myself two or three minutes to weigh my words before replying. I finally said, in substance: "There is only one thing for us to do and be just to both sides. We must use every means for a peaceful settlement of this difficulty. Let us be patient; let us continue to reason with the wilder element, even though some hotheads may

---

would survive. Those who resisted these policies and attempted to retain their tribal religions, languages, and cultures were called "traditionals."

threaten our lives. If the worst happens, however, it is our solemn duty to serve the United States government. Let no man ever say that we were disloyal! Following such a policy, dead or alive, we shall have no apology to make."

After the others had withdrawn, Sword informed me confidentially that certain young men had threatened to kill American Horse while asleep in his tent and that his friends had prevailed upon him and his wife to ask my hospitality for a few days. I showed Mrs. American Horse to a small room that I had vacant, and soon afterward came three strokes of the office bell—the signal for me to report at the agent's office.

I found there the agent, his chief clerk, and a visiting inspector, all of whom obviously regarded the situation as serious. "You see, Doctor," said the agent, "the occurrence of today was planned with remarkable accuracy, so that even our alert police were taken entirely by surprise and readily overpowered. What will be the sequel we cannot tell, but we must be prepared for anything. I shall be glad to have your views," he added.

I told him that I still did not believe there was any widespread plot or deliberate intention to make war upon the whites. In my own mind, I felt sure that the arrival of troops would be construed by the Ghost Dancers as a threat or a challenge, and would put them at once on the defensive. I was not in favor of that step; neither was Mr. Cook, who was also called into the conference; but the officials evidently feared a general uprising and argued that it was their duty to safeguard the lives of the employees and others by calling for the soldiers without more delay. Sword, Thunder Bear, and American Horse were sent for and their opinions appeared to be fully in accord with those of the agent and inspector, so the matter was given out as settled. As a matter of fact, the agent had telegraphed to Fort Robinson for troops before he made a pretense of consulting us Indians, and they were already on their way to Pine Ridge.

I scarcely knew at the time, but gradually learned afterward, that the Sioux had many grievances and causes for profound discontent, which lay back of and were more or less closely related to the Ghost Dance craze and the prevailing restlessness and excitement. Rations had been cut from time to time, the people were insufficiently fed, and their protests and appeals were disregarded. Never was more ruthless fraud and graft practiced upon a defenseless people than upon these poor natives by the politicians! Never were there more worthless "scraps of paper" anywhere in the world than many of the Indian treaties and government documents! Sickness was prevalent and the death rate alarming, especially among the children. Trouble from all these causes had for some time been developing but might have been checked by humane and conciliatory measures. The "Messiah craze" in itself was scarcely a source of danger, and one might almost as well call upon the army to suppress Billy

Sunday and his hysterical followers.[4] Other tribes than the Sioux who adopted the new religion were let alone, and the craze died a natural death in the course of a few months.

Among the leaders of the malcontents at this time were Jack Red Cloud, No Water, He Dog,[5] Four Bears, Yellow Bear, and Kicking Bear. Friendly leaders included American Horse, Young Man Afraid of His Horses, Bad Wound, Three Stars.[6] There was still another set whose attitude was not clearly defined, and among these men was Red Cloud, the greatest of them all.[7] He who had led his people so brilliantly and with such remarkable results, both in battle and diplomacy, was now an old man of over seventy years, living in a frame house which had been built for him within a

---

[4]William Ashley (Billy) Sunday (1862-1935) became a fundamentalist preacher renowned for his quite powerful and emotional sermons.

[5]No Water and He Dog were Oglala Lakota leaders.

[6]An influential Oglala Lakota leader, Young Man Afraid of His Horses was a progressive, as was Bad Wound. Charles Three Stars (Miniconjou) became an important source of information about the Sioux at the turn of the century.

[7]Red Cloud (Mahpiya-Luta, ca. 1822-1909) was the war leader and headman of the Oglala Lakota. In 1866, he planned the Sioux annihilation of Captain William J. Fetterman's command near Fort Kearney, Wyoming. Red Cloud forced the United States to abandon forts along the Bozeman Trail in northern Wyoming. An eloquent orator, he made many trips to Washington on behalf of his people. In 1878, he located on the Pine Ridge Reservation in western South Dakota. During his later years, younger warriors increasingly criticized his efforts to placate the government and his people.

half mile of the agency. He would come to council but said little or nothing. No one knew exactly where he stood, but it seemed that he was broken in spirit as in body and convinced of the hopelessness of his people's cause.

It was Red Cloud who asked the historic question, at a great council held in the Black Hills region with a government commission, and after Bishop Whipple had finished the invocation, "Which God is our brother praying to now? Is it the same God whom they have twice deceived, when they made treaties with us which they afterward broke?"

Early in the morning after the attempted arrest of Little, George rushed into my quarters and awakened me. "Come quick!" he shouted, "the soldiers are here!" I looked along the White Clay Creek toward the little railroad town of Rushville, Nebraska, twenty-five miles away, and just as the sun rose above the knife-edged ridges black with stunted pine, I perceived a moving black cloud of dust that marked the trail of the Ninth Cavalry. There was instant commotion among the camps of friendly Indians. Many women and children were coming to the agency for refuge, evidently fearing that the dreaded soldiers might attack their villages by mistake. Some who had not heard of their impending arrival hurried to the offices to ask what it meant. I assured those who had appealed to me that the troops were here only to preserve order, but their suspicions were not easily allayed.

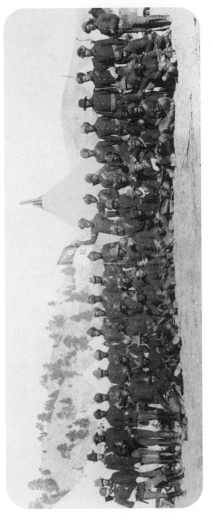

Troop K, Ninth Cavalry, African American troops known as the Buffalo Soldiers

Gen. Nelson A. Miles and his staff at Pine Ridge

As the cavalry came nearer, we saw that they were colored troopers who were wearing buffalo overcoats and muskrat caps; the Indians with quick wit called them buffalo soldiers.[8] They halted and established their temporary camp in the open space before the agency enclosure. The news had already gone out through the length and breadth of the reservation, and the wildest rumors were in circulation. Indian scouts might be seen upon every hilltop, closely watching the military encampment.

At this juncture came the startling news from Fort Yates, some 250 miles to the north of us, that Sitting Bull had been killed by Indian police while resisting arrest, and a number of his men with him, as well as several of the police. We next heard that the remnant of his band had fled in our direction and, soon afterward, that they had been joined by Big Foot's band from the western part of the Cheyenne River Agency,[9]

[8]From 1866 to 1900, the African American regiments, the Ninth and Tenth Cavalry and the Twenty-Fourth and Twenty-Fifth Infantries, served at military bases throughout the West. They fought against Indian tribes for twenty-five years. In addition, they tracked down outlaws and enforced order at miners' strikes. Between 1870 and 1890, fourteen African American soldiers from these regiments received the Congressional Medal of Honor for bravery.

[9]A traditional or "nonprogressive" Miniconjou Lakota leader, Big Foot and his people were located at Cheyenne River, South Dakota. After Sitting Bull was killed on 15 December 1890, his Hunkpapa Lakotas began to arrive in Big Foot's camp and joined the Miniconjou in the Ghost Dance. Although Big Foot had been a strong adherent of the Ghost Dance religion, he then disassociated himself from the religion. Aware that Gen. Nelson Miles

which lay directly in their road. United States troops continued to gather at strategic points, and of course the press seized upon the opportunity to enlarge upon the strained situation and predict an "Indian uprising." The reporters were among us and managed to secure much "news" that no one else ever heard of. Border towns were fortified, and cowboys and militia gathered in readiness to protect them against the "red devils." Certain classes of the frontier population industriously fomented the excitement for what there was in it for them, since much money is apt to be spent at such times. As for the poor Indians, they were quite as badly scared as the whites and perhaps with more reason.

General Brooke[10] undertook negotiations with the Ghost Dancers and finally induced them to come within reach. They encamped on a flat about a mile north of us and in full view, while the tractable bands were still gathered on the south and west. The large boarding school had locked its doors and succeeded in holding its hundreds of Indian children, partly for their own sakes and partly as hostages for the good behavior of their fathers. At the agency were now gathered all the government employees and their families, except such as had taken flight, together with traders,

---

wanted him arrested, the ailing Big Foot and his band of Miniconjou left Cheyenne River to join the "friendlies" at the Pine Ridge Agency.

[10]Gen. John S. Brooke commanded the troops sent to the Sioux agencies.

missionaries, and ranchmen, army officers, and newspaper men. It was a conglomerate population.

During this time of grave anxiety and nervous tension, the cooler heads among us went about our business and still refused to believe in the tragic possibility of an Indian war. It may be imagined that I was more than busy, though I had not such long distances to cover, for since many Indians accustomed to comfortable log houses were compelled to pass the winter in tents, there was even more sickness than usual. I had access and welcome to the camps of all the various factions, a privilege shared by my good friend Father Jutz, who was the Catholic missionary, and who was completely trusted by his people.

The Christmas season was fast approaching, and this is perhaps the brightest spot in the mission year. The children of the Sunday schools, and indeed all the people, look eagerly forward to the joyous feast; barrels and boxes are received and opened, candy bags made and filled, carols practiced, and churches decorated with ropes of spicy evergreen.

Anxious to relieve the tension in every way within his power, Mr. Cook and his helpers went on with their preparations upon even a larger scale than usual. Since all of the branch stations had been closed and the people called in, it was planned to keep the Christmas tree standing in the chapel for a week and to distribute gifts to a separate congregation each evening. I found myself pressed into the service and passed happy hours in the rectory. For me, at that critical

time, there was some inward struggle, as well as the
threat of outward conflict, and I could now recall what
my "white mother" [Mrs. Wood] had said jokingly,
referring to my pleasant friendships with many charming Boston girls. "I know one Sioux who has not been
conquered, and I shall not rest till he is captured."

I had planned to enter upon my life work unhampered by any other ties and declared that my love
should be vested in my people and my profession. At
last, however, I had met a woman whose sincerity was
convincing and whose ideals seemed very like my
own. Her childhood had been spent almost as much
out-of-doors as mine, on a lonely estate high up in the
Berkshire Hills; her ancestry Puritan on one side,
proud Tories on the other. She had been moved by
the appeals of that wonderful man, General Armstrong, and had gone to Hampton as a young girl to
teach the Indians there.[11] After three years, she undertook pioneer work in the West as teacher of a new
camp school among the wilder Sioux and, after much
travel and study of their peculiar problems, had been

[11]In 1868, the American Missionary Association of New York
opened Hampton Normal and Agricultural Institute, located near
Hampton, Virginia, as a school for freed slaves. Gen. Samuel
Chapman Armstrong (1839-93), a commander of Negro troops
during the Civil War and an agent of the Freedmen's Bureau, was
the founder and first principal. American Indian students were admitted in 1878 as an experiment in Indian Education. Impressed
by young Elaine Goodale when he visited her home at Sky Farm
in the summer of 1878, Armstrong later offered her a position at
Hampton. She joined the staff in the fall of 1883.

Mrs. Frank Wood, Eastman's "white mother"

From the Deep Woods to Civilization

Father Francis M. Craft, a Jesuit and missionary,
who was wounded during the massacre, 1891

offered the appointment she now held. She spoke the Sioux language fluently and went among the people with the utmost freedom and confidence. Her methods of work were very simple and direct. I do not know what unseen hand had guided me to her side, but on Christmas day of 1890, Elaine Goodale and I announced our engagement.

Three days later, we learned that Big Foot's band of Ghost Dancers from the Cheyenne River Reservation north of us was approaching the agency and that Major Whiteside[12] was in command of troops with orders to intercept them.

Late that afternoon, the Seventh Cavalry under Colonel Forsyth was called to the saddle and rode off toward Wounded Knee Creek, eighteen miles away. Father Craft, a Catholic priest who had some Indian blood and who knew Sitting Bull and his people, followed an hour or so later,[13] and I was much inclined to go too, but my fiancée pointed out that my duty lay rather at home with our Indians, and I stayed.

The morning of 29 December was sunny and pleasant. We were then all straining our ears toward

[12]Maj. Samuel Whiteside and troops from the Seventh Cavalry overtook Big Foot on 28 December. On Whiteside's recommendation, Big Foot and his band camped at Wounded Knee. Surrounded by 470 soldiers and 30 Indian scouts, the 106 warriors were separated from approximately 250 women and children.

[13]On the evening of the 28th, Col. James W. Forsyth, commander of the Seventh Cavalry, and his troops reinforced Whiteside and his soldiers at Wounded Knee. Accompanying him was Father Francis M. Craft, a missionary at Pine Ridge. A warrior stabbed and wounded Craft during the massacre.

Lakota Indians at Pine Ridge, ca. 1890

Big Foot's band of Miniconjou Lakota before Wounded Knee, ca. 1890

Wounded Knee, and about the middle of the forenoon, we distinctly heard the reports of the Hotchkiss guns.[14] Two hours later, a rider was seen approaching at full speed, and in a few minutes he had dismounted from his exhausted horse and handed his message to General Brooke's orderly. The Indians were watching their own messenger, who ran on foot along the northern ridges and carried the news to the so-called "hostile" camp. It was said that he delivered his message at almost the exact time as the mounted officer.

The resulting confusion and excitement was unmistakable. The white tepees disappeared as if by magic, and soon the caravans were in motion, going toward the natural fortress of the Badlands. In the "friendly" camp there was almost as much turmoil, and crowds of frightened women and children poured into the agency. Big Foot's band had been wiped out by the troops, and reprisals were naturally looked for. The enclosure was not barricaded in any way, and we had but a small detachment of troops for our protection. Sentinels were placed, and machine guns trained on the various approaches.

A few hot-headed young braves fired on the sentinels and wounded two of them. The Indian police began to answer by shooting at several braves who were apparently about to set fire to some of the outly-

[14]Developed in 1878, the Hotchkiss machine gun was a hand-cranked weapon capable of firing fifty two-pound shells per minute. At Wounded Knee, four Hotchkiss guns fired on Big Foot and his band.

ing buildings. Every married employee was seeking a place of safety for his family, the interpreter among them. Just then General Brooke ran out into the open, shouting at the top of his voice to the police: "Stop, stop! Doctor, tell them they must not fire until ordered!" I did so, as the bullets whistled by us, and the general's coolness perhaps saved all our lives, for we were in no position to repel a large attacking force. Since we did not reply, the scattered shots soon ceased, but the situation remained critical for several days and nights.

My office was full of refugees. I called one of my good friends and asked him to saddle my two horses and stay by them. "When general fighting begins, take them to Miss Goodale and see her to the railroad if you can," I told him. Then I went over to the rectory. Mrs. Cook refused to go without her husband, and Miss Goodale would not leave while there was a chance of being of service. The house was crowded with terrified people, most of them Christian Indians, whom our friends were doing their best to pacify.

At dusk, the Seventh Cavalry returned with their twenty-five dead and I believe thirty-four wounded, most of them by their own comrades, who had encircled the Indians, while few of the latter had guns.[15] A majority of the thirty or more Indians wounded were

[15]On the morning of 29 December, Forsyth ordered Big Foot's band to disarm. Black Coyote, deaf and possibly mentally ill, refused to turn in his weapon without being compensated. As the soldiers tried to take his weapon, a shot was fired and a massacre

women and children, including babies in their arms. As there were not tents enough for all, Mr. Cook offered us the mission chapel, in which the Christmas tree still stood, for a temporary hospital. We tore out the pews and covered the floor with hay and quilts. There we laid the poor creatures side by side in rows, and the night was devoted to caring for them as best we could. Many were frightfully torn by pieces of shells, and the suffering was terrible. General Brooke placed me in charge, and I had to do nearly all the work, for although the army surgeons were more than ready to help as soon as their own men had been cared for, the tortured Indians would scarcely allow a man in uniform to touch them. Mrs. Cook, Miss Goodale, and several of Mr. Cook's Indian helpers acted as volunteer nurses. In spite of all our efforts, we lost the greater part of them, but a few recovered, including several children who had lost all their relatives and who were adopted into kind Christian families.

On the day following the Wounded Knee massacre there was a blizzard, in the midst of which I was ordered out with several Indian police, to look for a policeman who was reported to have been wounded and left some two miles from the agency. We did not find him. This was the only time during the whole affair that I carried a weapon; a friend lent me a revolver,

----

ensued. During the massacre, 146 Indians were killed (including forty-four women and eighteen children). Twenty-five soldiers died and thirty-nine were wounded.

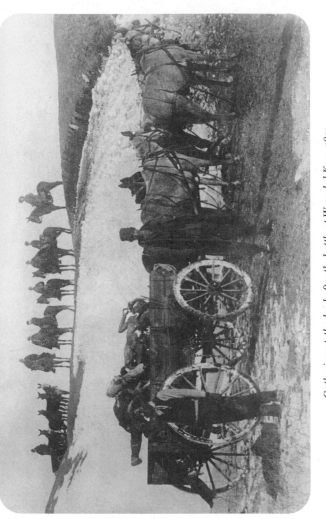

Gathering up the dead after the battle at Wounded Knee, 1891

Courtesy Minnesota Historical Society

x

235

Soldiers bury the dead after Wounded Knee, 1891

which I put in my overcoat pocket, and it was lost on the ride. On the third day[16] it cleared, and the ground was covered with an inch or two of fresh snow. We had feared that some of the Indian wounded might have been left on the field, and a number of us volunteered to go and see. I was placed in charge of the expedition of about a hundred civilians, ten or fifteen of whom were white men. We were supplied with wagons in which to convey any whom we might find still alive. Of course, a photographer and several reporters were of the party.

Fully three miles from the scene of the massacre we found the body of a woman completely covered with a blanket of snow, and from this point on we found them scattered along as they had been relentlessly hunted down and slaughtered while fleeing for their lives. Some of our people discovered relatives or friends among the dead, and there was much wailing and mourning. When we reached the spot where the Indian camp had stood, among the fragments of burned tents and other belongings we saw the frozen bodies lying close together or piled upon one another. I counted eighty bodies of men who had been in the council and who were almost as helpless as the women and babes when the firing began, for nearly all their guns had been taken from them. A reckless and desperate young Indian had fired the first shot when

[16]On the third day: On 1 January 1891, Eastman led an expedition to try to find survivors.

the search for weapons was well under way. Immediately the troops opened fire from all sides, killing not only unarmed men, women, and children but their own comrades who stood opposite them, for the camp was entirely surrounded.

It took all of my nerve to keep my composure in the face of this spectacle and of the excitement and grief of my Indian companions, nearly every one of whom was crying aloud or singing his death song. The white men became very nervous, but I set them to examining and uncovering every body to see if any were living. Although they had been lying untended in the snow and cold for two days and nights, a number had survived. Among them I found a baby of about a year old warmly wrapped and entirely unhurt. I brought her in, and she was afterward adopted and educated by an army officer. One man who was severely wounded begged me to fill his pipe. When we brought him into the chapel, he was welcomed by his wife and daughters with cries of joy, but he died a day or two later.

Under a wagon I discovered an old woman, totally blind and entirely helpless. A few had managed to crawl away to some place of shelter, and we found in a log store nearby several who were badly hurt and others who had died after reaching there. After we had dispatched several wagonloads to the agency, we observed groups of warriors watching us from adjacent buttes; probably friends of the victims, who had come there for the same purpose. A majority of our

Exterior of the Chapel of the Holy Cross at Pine Ridge Agency, 1891

Interior of the chapel, which was converted to serve as a hospital after the massacre, 1891

Wounded Indians being treated in the chapel hospital, 1891

Grand Council of American Indian chiefs meets at Pine Ridge, 1891

Courtesy Minnesota Historical Society

party, fearing an attack, insisted that someone ride back to the agency for an escort of soldiers, and as mine was the best horse, it fell to me to go. I covered the eighteen miles in quick time and was not interfered with in any way, although if the Indians had meant mischief, they could easily have picked me off from any of the ravines and gulches.

All this was a severe ordeal for me who had so lately put all his faith in the Christian love and lofty ideals of the white man. Yet I passed no hasty judgment and was thankful that I might be of some service and relieve even a small part of the suffering. An appeal published in a Boston paper brought us liberal supplies of much-needed clothing and linen for dressings. Bishop Hare of South Dakota visited us and was overcome by faintness when he entered his mission chapel, thus transformed into a rude hospital.

After some days of extreme tension, and weeks of anxiety, the "hostiles," so called, were at last induced to come in and submit to a general disarmament. Father Jutz, the Catholic missionary, had gone bravely among them and used all his influence toward a peaceful settlement. The troops were all recalled and took part in a grand review before General Miles,[17] no doubt intended to impress us with their superior force.

[17]Gen. Nelson A. Miles (1839-1925) won many victories against the Sioux during his 1876-77 winter campaign on the Northern Plains. He also intercepted the fleeing Nez Perce and forced their surrender in 1877. Miles captured Geronimo in 1886. Four years later, he commanded the Military Division of the Missouri and directed the concentration of troops in South Dakota.

In March, all being quiet, Miss Goodale decided to send in her resignation and go east to visit her relatives, and our wedding day was set for the following June.

He favored military control over the Sioux. Outraged by the deaths of women and children at Wounded Knee, Miles removed Colonel Forsyth from command.

XX

War with the Politicians

WHEN THE most industrious and advanced Indians on the reservation, to the number of thousands, were ordered into camp within gunshot of Pine
Ridge Agency, they had necessarily left their homes,
their livestock, and most of their household belongings unguarded. In all troubles between the two races,
history tells us that the innocent and faithful Indians
have been sufferers, and this case was no exception.
There was much sickness from exposure, and much
unavoidable sorrow and anxiety. Furthermore, the
"war" being over, these loyal Indians found that their
houses had been entered and pillaged, and many of
their cattle and horses had disappeared.

The authorities laid all this at the door of the "hostiles," and no doubt in some cases the charge may have
been true. On the other hand, this was a golden opportunity for white horse and cattle thieves in the surrounding country; ranch owners within a radius of a
hundred miles claimed large losses also. Moreover,
the government herd of "Issue cattle"[1] was found to be
greatly depleted. It was admitted that some had been
killed for food by those Indians who fled in terror to

---

[1]Issue cattle: Cattle to be distributed to the Indians.

the Badlands, but only a limited number could be accounted for in this way, and little of the stolen property was ever found. An inspector was ordered to examine and record these "depredation claims," and Congress passed a special appropriation of $100,000 to pay them. We shall hear more of this later.

I have tried to make it clear that there was no "Indian outbreak" in 1890-91 and that such trouble as we had may justly be charged to the dishonest politicians, who through unfit appointees first robbed the Indians, then bullied them, and finally in a panic called for troops to suppress them. From my first days at Pine Ridge, certain Indians and white people had taken every occasion to whisper into my reluctant ears the tale of wrongs, real or fancied, committed by responsible officials on the reservation, or by their connivance. To me these stories were unbelievable from the point of view of common decency. I held that a great government such as ours would never condone or permit any such practices. At that time, I had not dreamed what American politics really is, and I had the most exalted admiration of our noted public men. Accordingly, I dismissed these reports as mere gossip or the inventions of mischief-makers.

In March 1891, I was invited to address the Congregational Club of Chicago, and on my arrival in the city, I found to my surprise that the press still fostered the illusion of a general Indian uprising in the spring. It was reported that all the towns adjoining the Sioux reservations had organized and were regularly drilling a home guard for their protection. These alarmists seemed either ignorant or forgetful of the fact that there were only about 30,000 Sioux altogether, or perhaps 6,000 men of fighting age, more than half of whom had been civilized and Christianized for a generation and had just proved their loyalty and steadfastness through a trying time. Furthermore, the leaders of the late "hostiles" were even then in confinement in Fort Sheridan. When I was approached by the reporters, I reminded them of this and said that everything was quiet in the field, but if there were any danger from the Ghost Dancers, Chicago was in the most immediate peril!

Fortunately we had in the office of commissioner of Indian affairs at that time a sincere man, and one who was deeply in sympathy with educational and missionary work, General Morgan of Indiana.[2] He was a lover of fair play, and throughout my fight for justice, he gave me all the support within his power. As I have before intimated, I found at Pine Ridge no conveyance for the doctor's professional use, and indeed no medical equipment worthy the name. The agency doctor was thrown entirely upon his own resources, without the support of colleagues, and there was no serious attempt at sanitation or preventive work. I had spent a good part of my salary, as well as funds contributed by

[2]A Baptist educator, Gen. Thomas Jefferson Morgan (1839-1902) supported the Indian Rights Movement and advocated the assimilation of Indians. From 1889 to 1893, he was commissioner of Indian affairs.

friends for the purpose, in the purchase of suitable medical supplies and instruments. Finally, I boldly asked for a team and buggy, also a hospital for critical cases, with a trained nurse, and a house for us to live in. Somewhat to my surprise, all of these were allowed. I was ambitious to give efficient service, so far as it was possible, and I loved my work, though the field was too large and the sick were too many for one man to care for, and there were many obstacles in the way. One was the native prejudice, still strong, against the white man's medicine, and especially against any kind of surgical operation. The people were afraid of anesthesia, and even in the cases where life depended on it, they had steadfastly refused to allow a limb to be amputated. If I so much as put on a plaster cast, I had no sooner left our temporary hospital than they took it off.

It may be of interest to tell how this prejudice was in part overcome. One day my friend Three Stars, a Christian chief, came in with his wife, who had dislocated her shoulder. "Can you help her?" he asked. "Yes," I said, "but I must first put her to sleep. You should have brought her to me last night, when it first happened," I added, "and then that would not have been necessary."

"You know best," replied Three Stars. "I leave it entirely with you." In the presence of a number of the wounded Indians, I administered a small quantity of chloroform and jerked the arm back into its socket. She came back to consciousness laughing. It appeared to them a miracle, and I was appealed to after that whenever I dressed a painful wound, to "give me some of that stuff you gave to Three Stars's wife."

Not long afterwards, I amputated the leg of a mixed-blood, which had been terribly crushed, and he not only recovered perfectly but was soon able to get about with ease on the artificial limb that I procured for him. My reputation was now established. I had gained much valuable experience, and in this connection I want to express my appreciation of the kindness of several army surgeons with whom it was my pleasure to work, one of whom took my place during a six weeks' leave of absence, when I went east to be married.

I had some interesting experiences with the Indian conjurers, or "medicine men," to use the names commonly given. I would rather say, mental healer or Christian Scientist of our day, for the medicine man was all of that, and further he practiced massage or osteopathy, used the Turkish bath, and some useful vegetable remedies. But his main hold on the minds of the people was gained through his appeals to the spirits and his magnetic and hypnotic powers.

I was warned that these men would seriously hamper my work, but I succeeded in avoiding antagonism by a policy of friendliness. Even when brought face-to-face with them in the homes of my patients, I preserved a professional and brotherly attitude. I recall one occasion when a misunderstanding between the parents of a sick child had resulted in a double call.

The father, who was a policeman and a good friend of mine, urgently requested me to see his child, while the frantic mother sent for the most noted of the medicine men.

"Brother," I said, when I found him already in attendance, "I am glad you got here first. I had a long way to come, and the child needs immediate attention."

"I think so, too," he replied, "but now that you are here, I will withdraw."

"Why so? Surely two doctors should be better than one," I retorted. "Let us consult together. In the first place, we must determine what ails the child. Then we will decide upon the treatment." He seemed pleased, and I followed up on the suggestion of a consultation by offering to enter with him the sweat bath he had prepared as a means of purification before beginning his work. After that, I had no difficulty in getting his consent to my treatment of the patient, and in time he became one of my warm friends. It was not unusual for him and other conjurers to call at my office to consult me or "borrow" my medicine.

I had some of the wounded in my care all winter. I remember one fine-looking man who was severely injured; a man of ordinary strength would have succumbed, but yet his strength and courage were exceptional, and best of all, he had perfect faith in my ability to restore him to health. All through those months of trial, his pretty young wife was my faithful assistant. Every morning she came to see him with her

Charles Eastman and Elaine Goodale
just prior to their marriage, 1891

baby on her back, cheering him and inspiring us both to do our best. When at last he was able to travel, they came together to say good-bye. She handed me something, carefully wrapped in paper, and asked me not to open it until they had gone. When I did so, I found that she had cut off her beautiful long braids of hair and given them to me in token of her gratitude!

I was touched by this little illustration of woman's devotion and happy in the thought that I was soon to realize my long dream—to become a complete man! I thought of little else than the good we two could do together and was perfectly contented with my salary of $1,200 a year. In spite of all that I had gone through, life was not yet a serious matter to me. I had faith in everyone and accepted civilization and Christianity at their face value—a great mistake, as I was to learn later on. I had come back to my people, not to minister to their physical needs alone, but to be a missionary in every sense of the word. I was much struck with the loss of manliness and independence in these, the first "reservation Indians" I had ever known. I longed above all things to help them to regain their self-respect.

On 18 June 1891, I was married to Elaine Goodale in the Church of the Ascension, New York City, by the Reverend Doctor Donald. Her two sisters were bridesmaids, and I had my chum in the medical school for best man, and two Dartmouth classmates as ushers.

After the wedding breakfast held in her father's

apartments, we went to Sky Farm, my wife's birthplace in the lovely Berkshire Hills, where she and her sister Dora, as little girls, wrote the *Apple Blossoms* and other poems. A reception was given for us at Dorchester by Mr. and Mrs. Wood, and after attending the Wellesley College commencement and spending a few days with my wife's family, we returned to the West by way of Montreal. At Flandreau, South Dakota, my brother John had gathered all the family and a whole band of Flandreau Sioux to welcome us. There my father had brought me home from Canada, an absolute wild Indian, only eighteen years earlier! My honored father had been dead for some years, but my brothers had arranged to have a handsome memorial to him erected and unveiled at this time.

Our new home was building when we reached Pine Ridge, and we started life together in the old barracks, while planning the finishing and furnishing of the new. It was ready for us early in fall. I had gained permission to add an open fireplace and a few other homelike touches at my own expense. We had the chiefs and leading men to dine with us, and quite as often some of the humbler Indians and poor old women were our guests. In fact, we kept open house, and the people loved to come and talk with us in their own tongue. My wife accompanied me on many of my trips now that I had a carriage, and she was always prepared with clean clothing, bandages, and nourishing food for my needy patients.

There was nothing I called my own save my dogs

and horses and my medicine bags, yet I was perfectly happy, for I had not only gained the confidence of my people but that of the white residents, and even the border ranchmen called me in now and then. I answered every call and have ridden forty or fifty miles in a blizzard, over dangerous roads, sometimes at night, while my young wife suffered much more than I in the anxiety with which she awaited my return. That was a bitterly cold winter, I remember, and we had only wood fires (soft wood) and no "modern conveniences"; yet we kept in perfect health. The year rolled around and our first child was born—a little girl whom we called Dora.

Meanwhile, though the troops had been recalled, we were under heavy military agents; there were several changes, and our relations were pleasant with them all. The time came for the small annual payment of treaty money, and $100,000 payment for depredation claims, of which I have spoken, was also to be made by a special disbursing agent. This payment was not made by check, as usual, but in cash, and I was asked to be one of the three witnesses. I told the special agent that, as I was almost constantly occupied, it would be impossible for me to witness the payment, which would take several days. But he assured me that if only one of the three were present at a time, it would be sufficient, and, understanding my duties to be only nominal, I consented.

I was in the office from time to time while the payment was going on. I saw the people sign their names, generally by mark, on the roll that had been prepared, opposite the amount each was supposed to receive. Then a clerk at another desk handed each in turn a handful of silver and bills. But, the money was not counted out to him, and he was given no chance to count it until he got outside. Even then, many could not count it and did not clearly understand how much it ought to be, while the traders and others were close at hand to get all or part of it without delay.

Before I knew it, I was approached by one and another, who declared that they had not received the full amount, and I found that in numerous cases reliable persons had counted the cash as soon as the payees came out of the office. A very able white teacher, a college graduate, counted for several old people who were protégés of hers; an influential native minister did the same, and so did several others. All reported that the amount was short from 10 percent to 15 percent. When anyone brought a shortage to the attention of the disbursing agent or his clerk, he was curtly told that he had made a mistake or lost some of the money.

The complaints grew louder, and other suspicious circumstances were reported. Within a few days it was declared that an investigation would be ordered. The agent who had made the payment and immediately left the agency, being informed of the situation, came back and tried to procure affidavits to show that it had been an honest payment. He urged me to sign as one of the original witnesses, arguing that I had already committed myself. I refused. I said, "After all, I did not see the full amount paid to each claimant. As the payment was conducted, it was impossible for me to do so. I trusted you; therefore, I allowed you to use my name, but I don't care to sign again."

The regular agent in charge of our Indians at the time was, as I have said, an army officer, with military ideas of discipline. Like myself, he had been in the field much of the time while the payment was going on but had officially vouched for its correctness and signed all the papers, and he took his stand upon this. He remonstrated with me for my position in the matter and did his best to avoid an investigation. But I was convinced that a gross fraud had been committed, and in my inexperience I believed that it had only to be exposed to be corrected. I determined to do all in my power to secure justice for those poor, helpless people, even though it must appear that I was careless in signing the original papers.

I added my protest to that of the others, and the department sent out a Quaker, an inspector whose record was excellent and who went about the work in a direct and straightforward way. He engaged a reliable interpreter and called in witnesses on both sides. At the end of a fortnight, he reported that about $10,000 had been dishonestly withheld from the Indians. A few of the better-educated and more influential, especially mixed-bloods, had been paid in full while the old and ignorant had lost as high as 15 percent or 20 percent of their money. Evidence in support of this decision was sent to Washington.

After a short interval, I learned with astonishment that the report of this trusted inspector had not been accepted by the secretary of the interior, who had ordered a second investigation to supersede the first. Naturally, the second investigation was a farce and quickly ended in "whitewashing" the special payment. The next step was to punish those who had testified for the Indians or tried to bring about an honest investigation in the face of official opposition. Of these, I had been perhaps the most active and outspoken.

The usual method of disciplining agency Indians in such a case is to deprive them of various privileges, possibly of rations also, and sometimes to imprison them on trivial pretexts. White men with Indian wives, and missionaries, may be ordered off the reservation as "disturbers of the peace," while with the government employees, some grounds are usually found for their dismissal from the service.

I was promptly charged with "insubordination" and other things. But my good friend, General Morgan, then commissioner, declined to entertain the charges. I, on my part, kept up the fight at Washington through influential friends and made every effort to prove my case, or rather, the case of the people, for I had at no time any personal interest in the payment. The local authorities followed the usual tactics and undertook to force a resignation by making my position at Pine Ridge intolerable. An Indian agent has almost autocratic power, and the conditions of life on an agency are such as to make every resident largely dependent upon his goodwill. We soon found ourselves hampered in our work and harassed by every imaginable annoyance. My requisitions were overlooked or "forgotten," and it became difficult to secure the necessaries of life. I would receive a curt written order to proceed without delay to some remote point to visit a certain alleged patient; then, before I had covered the distance, would be overtaken by a mounted policeman with arbitrary orders to return at once to the agency. On driving in rapidly and reporting to the agent's office for details of the supposed emergency, I might be rebuked for overdriving the horses and charged with neglect of some chronic case of which I had either never been informed or to which it had been physically impossible for me to give regular attention.

This sort of thing went on for several months, and I was finally summoned to Washington for a personal conference. I think I may safely say that my story was believed by Senators Dawes and Hoar,[3] and also by

[3]Henry Laurens Dawes (1816-1903), a Republican from Massachusetts, was a staunch assimilationist. Between 1857 and 1893, Dawes served in both the House of Representatives and the Senate. As chairman of the Senate Committee on Indian Affairs, he was primarily responsible for preparing the Dawes Severalty Act (1887). It distributed tribal land to individual Indian males and gave citizenship to those who accepted allotments. (For a more complete discussion of the Dawes Severalty Act, see fn. 9 in Chapter XXII.) George Frisbie Hoar (1826-1904) was a U.S. senator from Massachusetts from 1877-1904.

A Sioux delegation to Washington, D.C., Winter 1891. Left to right: (first row) High Hawk, Fire Lightning, Little Wound, Two Strike, Young Man Afraid of His Horses, Spotted Elk, Big Road; (second row) F.D. Lewis, He Dog, Spotted Horse, American Horse, George Sword, Louis Shangreau, Bat Pourier; (third row) Dave Zephier, Hump, High Pipe, Fast Thunder, Rev. Charles Cook, P.T. Johnson

Commissioner Morgan. I also saw the secretary of the interior and the president, but they were noncommittal. On my return, the same inspector who had whitewashed the payment was directed to investigate the "strained relation" between the agent and myself. My wife, who had meantime published several very frank letters in influential eastern papers, was made a party in this case.

I will not dwell upon the farcical nature of this "investigation." The inspector was almost openly against us from the start, and the upshot of the affair was that I was shortly offered a transfer. The agent could not be dislodged, and my position had become impossible. The superintendent of the boarding school, a clergyman, and one or two others who had fought on our side were also forced to leave. We had many other warm sympathizers who could not speak out without risking their livelihood.

We declined to accept the compromise, being utterly disillusioned and disgusted with these revelations of government mismanagement in the field and realizing the helplessness of the best-equipped Indians to secure a fair deal for their people. Later experience, both my own and that of others, has confirmed me in this view. Had it not been for strong friends in the East and on the press, and the unusual boldness and disregard of personal considerations with which we had conducted the fight, I could not have lasted a month. All other means failing, these men will not hesitate to manufacture evidence against a man's or a woman's personal reputation in order to attain their ends.

It was a great disappointment to us both to give up our plans of work and our first home, to which we had devoted much loving thought and most of our little means; but it seemed to us then the only thing to do. We had not the heart to begin the same thing over again elsewhere. I resigned my position in the Indian service and removed with my family to the city of St. Paul, where I proposed to enter upon the independent practice of medicine.[4]

[4]This section refers to Eastman's dispute with Capt. George LeRoy Brown, acting Indian agent, and James A. Cooper, special agent. Cooper had been appointed to disburse the $100,000 congressional appropriation for the "nonhostile" Sioux at Pine Ridge. When Indians complained that they were not receiving their rightful share, Charles and Elaine Eastman informed their friends rather than Agent Brown. Between May 1892 and January 1893, charges flew back and forth. Brown persuaded Commissioner Thomas J. Morgan to offer Eastman transfers to other posts, which Eastman rejected. In January 1893, Secretary of the Interior John Noble ordered Morgan to notify Eastman that he should report to Noble in Washington. By 23 January, Eastman had returned to Pine Ridge. Two days later, Secretary Noble wrote Morgan that Eastman should be suspended unless he was reassigned or appointed to another place. Despite his respect for Eastman, Noble further ordered that if the doctor refused, Eastman must resign. Eastman replied, "I prefer to resign."

XXI

Civilization as Preached and Practiced

AFTER thirty years of exile from the land of my nativity and the home of my ancestors, I came back to Minnesota in 1893. My mother was born on the shores of Lake Harriet; my great-grandfather's village is now a part of the beautiful park system of the city of Minneapolis.

I came to St. Paul with very little money, for one cannot save much out of $100 a month, and we had been compelled to sacrifice nearly all that we had spent on our little home. It was midwinter, and our baby daughter was only eight months old, but our courage was good nevertheless. I had to wait for the regular state medical examination before being admitted to practice, as Minnesota was one of the first states to pass such a law, and the examinations were searching and covered three days' time. If I remember rightly, there were some forty-five applicants who took them with me, and I was told that nearly half of them failed to pass. It was especially hard on country practitioners who had practiced successfully for many years but were weak in theory of medicine along certain lines.

Although a young couple in a strange city, we were cordially received socially, and while we were seriously handicapped by lack of means, we determined to win out. I opened an office, hung out my sign, and waited for patients. It was the hardest work I had ever done! Most of the time we were forced to board for the sake of economy, and were hard put to it to meet office rent and our modest living expenses. At this period I was peculiarly tried with various temptations, by yielding to which it seemed that I could easily relieve myself from financial strain. I was persistently solicited for illegal practice, and this by persons who were not only intelligent, but apparently of good social standing. In their fear of exposure, they were ready to go to large expense and were astonished when I refused to consider anything of the sort. A large number came to me for Indian medicine and treatment. I told them, of course, that I had no such medicine. Again, one of the best known "doctors" of this class in the Northwest invited me to go into partnership with him. Finally, a prominent businessman of St. Paul offered to back me up financially if I would put up an "Indian medicine" sign under my own name, assuring me that there was a "fortune in it."

To be sure, I had been bitterly disappointed in the character of the United States Army and the honor of government officials. Still, I had seen the better side of civilization, and I determined that the good men and women who had helped me should not be betrayed. The Christ ideal might be radical, visionary, even impractical, as judged in the light of my later experiences; it still seemed to me logical and in line with most of my Indian training. My heart was still strong, and I had the continual inspiration of a brave comrade at my side.

With all the rest, I was deeply regretful of the work that I had left behind. I could not help thinking that if the president knew, if the good people of this country knew, of the wrong, it would yet be righted. I had not seen half of the savagery of civilization! While I had plenty of leisure, I began to put upon paper some of my earliest recollections, with the thought that our children might some day like to read of that wilderness life. When my wife discovered what I had written, she insisted upon sending it to *St. Nicholas*. Much to my surprise, the sketches were immediately accepted and appeared during the following year. This was the beginning of my first book, *Indian Boyhood*, which was not completed until several years later.

We were slowly gaining ground, when one day a stranger called on me in my office. He was, as I learned, one of the field secretaries of the International Committee of YMCA and had apparently called to discuss the feasibility of extending this movement among the Indians. After we had talked for some time, he broached the plan of putting a man into the Indian field and ended by urging me to consider taking up the work. My first thought was that it was out of the question to sacrifice my profession and practice at this juncture, when I was just getting a promising start. Then, too, I doubted my fitness for religious work. He still pressed me to accept, and he pointed out the far-reaching importance of this new step, and declared that they had not been able to hear of anyone else of my race so well-fitted to undertake it. We took the matter under consideration, and with some reluctance I agreed to organize the field if they would meantime educate a young Indian whom I would name to be my successor. I had in mind the thought that when the man I had chosen graduated from the International Training School at Springfield, Massachusetts, I could again return to my practice.

I selected Arthur Tibbets, a Sioux, who was duly graduated in three years, when I resigned in his favor. I had been unable to keep an office in St. Paul, where we made our home, but I carried my small medical case with me on all my trips and was often appealed to by the Indians for my professional help. I traveled over a large part of the western states and in Canada, visiting the mission stations among Indians of all tribes and organizing young men's associations wherever conditions permitted. I think I organized some forty-three associations. This gave me a fine opportunity to study Protestant missionary effort among Indians. I seriously considered the racial attitude toward God[1] and almost unconsciously reopened the book of my early religious training. I asked myself how it was that our simple lives were so imbued with the spirit of worship, while much churchgoing among white and

---

[1]The racial attitude that Eastman may refer to is that most cultural groups worship a supreme deity in their own image.

Christian Indians led often to such very small results.

A new point of view came to me then and there. This latter was a machine-made religion. It was supported by money, and more money could only be asked for on the showing made; therefore, too many of the workers were after quantity rather than quality of religious experience.

I was constantly meeting with groups of young men of the Sioux, Cheyennes, Crees, Ojibways, and others, in log cabins or little frame chapels, and trying to set before them in simple language the life and character of the Man Jesus. I was cordially received everywhere and always listened to with the closest attention. Curiously enough, even among these men who sought light on the white man's ideals, the racial philosophy emerged from time to time.

I remember one old battle-scarred warrior who sat among the young men and got up and said, in substance: "Why, we have followed this law you speak of for untold ages! We owned nothing, because everything is from Him. Food was free, land free as sunshine and rain. Who has changed all this? The white man; and yet he says he is a believer in God! He does not seem to inherit any of the traits of his Father, nor does he follow the example set by his brother Christ."

Another of the older men had attentively followed our Bible study and attended every meeting for a whole week. I finally called upon him for his views. After a long silence he said:

"I have come to the conclusion that this Jesus was

an Indian. He was opposed to material acquirement and to great possessions. He was inclined to peace. He was as unpractical as any Indian and set no price upon his labor of love. These are not the principles upon which the white man has founded his civilization. It is strange that he could not rise to these simple principles commonly observed among our people."

These words put the spell of an uncomfortable silence upon our company, but it did not appear that the old man had intended any sarcasm or unkindness, for after a minute he added that he was glad we had selected such an unusual character for our model.

At the Crow Agency I met a Scotsman, a missionary of fine type, who was doing good work. This man told me a strange story of his conversion. As a young man, he had traveled extensively in this and other countries. He spent one winter at Manitoba, near an Indian reservation, and there he met a young Indian who had been converted by one of his own tribesmen and was intensely interested in the life of Christ. This young man was a constant reader in his Indian Bible, and he talked of Christ so eloquently and so movingly as to cause serious thought on the part of the traveler. To make a long story short, he finally went home to Scotland and studied for the ministry and then returned to America to enter the field of Indian missions. It happened that the young Indian who made so deep an impression on his white friend was my own uncle, who had been baptized Joseph Eastman.

My two uncles who were in the Custer fight lived in Canada from the time of our flight in 1862, and both died there. I was happy to be sent to that part of the country in time to see the elder one alive. He had been a father to me up to the age of fifteen, and I had not seen him for over twenty years. I found him a farmer, living in a Christian community. I had sent word in advance of my coming, and my uncle's family had made of it a great occasion. All of my old playmates were there. My uncle was so happy that tears welled up in his eyes. "When we are old," he smiled, "our hearts are not strong in moments like this. The Great Spirit has been kind to let me see my boy again before I die." The early days were recalled as we feasted together. We all agreed that the chances were I should have been killed before reaching the age of twenty if I had remained among them; for, said they, I was very anxious to emulate my uncle, who had been a warrior of great reputation. Afterward, I visited the grave of my grandmother, whose devotion had meant so much to me as a motherless child. This was one of the great moments of my life.

Throughout this period of my work I was happy, being unhampered by official red tape in the effort to improve conditions among my people. The superintendent of Indian affairs in Manitoba was very kind and gave me every facility to go among the Indians. He asked me to make a comparative report on their condition on both sides of the border, but this I declined to undertake, unwilling to prejudice the government officials under whom I must carry on my work in the United States.

Another trip took me among the Ojibways, who used to take many a Sioux scalp, while we prized an eagle feather earned in battle with them. But those who had actually engaged in warlike exploits were now old and much inclined toward a peaceful life. I met some very able native preachers among them. I also visited for the first time the "Five Civilized Tribes" of the Indian Territory, now the state of Oklahoma.[2] As is well known, these people intermarried largely among the whites and had their own governments, schools, and thriving towns. When I appeared at Tahlequah, the Cherokee capital, the Senate took a recess in honor of their Sioux visitor. At Bacone College[3] I addressed the students, and at the Cherokee male and female seminaries. It was an odd coincidence that at the latter school I found one of the young ladies in the act of reading an essay on my wife, Elaine Goodale Eastman!

Among other duties of my position, I was expected to make occasional speaking trips through the East to

[2]Eastman refers to the Cherokee, Muscogee-Creek, Chickasaw, Choctaw, and Seminole. These Southeastern tribes were forcibly removed to Indian Territory during the 1830s. They were called "Civilized" because many of them adopted Christianity, American education, and commercial agriculture.

[3]Bacone College was in Muskogee, Oklahoma. In 1851, the Oklahoma Cherokee established male and female seminaries, where Cherokee students studied a curriculum based on that of Mount Holyoke Seminary in Massachusetts.

arouse interest in the work, and it thus happened that I addressed large audiences in Chicago, New York, Boston, and at Lake Mohonk. I was taken by slum and settlement workers to visit the slums and dives of the cities, which gave another shock to my ideals of "Christian civilization." Of course, I had seen something of the poorer parts of Boston during my medical course, but not at night, and not in a way to realize the horror and wretchedness of it as I did now. To be sure, I had been taught even as a child that there are always some evil-minded men in every nation, and we knew well what it is to endure physical hardship, but our poor lost nothing of their self-respect and dignity. Our great men not only divided their last kettle of food with a neighbor, but if great grief should come to them, such as the death of child or wife, they would voluntarily give away their few possessions and begin life over again in token of their sorrow. We could not conceive of the extremes of luxury and misery existing thus side by side, for it was common observation with us that the coarse weeds, if permitted to grow, will choke out the more delicate flowers. Yet I still held before my race the highest, and as yet unattained, ideals of the white man.

One of the strongest rebukes I ever received from an Indian for my acceptance of these ideals and philosophy was administered by an old chief of the Sac and Fox tribe in Iowa. I was invited to visit them by the churches of Toledo and Tama City, which were much concerned by the absolute refusal of this small tribe to accept civilization and Christianity. I surmise that these good people hoped to use me as an example of the benefits of education for the Indian.

I was kindly received at their village and made, as I thought, a pretty good speech, emphasizing the necessity of educating their children and urging their acceptance of the Christian religion. The old chief rose to answer. He was glad that I had come to visit them. He was also glad that I was apparently satisfied with the white man's religion and civilization. As for them, he said, neither of these had seemed good to them. The white man had showed neither respect for nature nor reverence toward God but, he thought, tried to buy God with the by-products of nature. He tried to buy his way into heaven, but he did not even know where heaven is.

"As for us," he concluded, "we shall still follow the old trail. If you should live long, and some day the Great Spirit shall permit you to visit us again, you will find us still Indians, eating with wooden spoons out of bowls of wood. I have done."

I was even more impressed a few minutes later, when one of his people handed me my pocketbook containing my railway tickets and a considerable sum of money. I had not known I lost it and had not even missed it! I said to the state missionary who was at my side, "Better let these Indians alone! If I had lost my money in the streets of your Christian city, I should probably have never seen it again."

XXII

At the Nation's Capital

M Y WORK for the International Committee of Young Men's Christian Associations[1] brought me into close association with some of the best products of American civilization. I believe that such men as Richard Morse, John R. Mott, Wilbur Messer, Charles Ober[2] and his brother, and others have, through their organization and personal influence, contributed vitally to the stability and well-being of the nation. Among the men on the International Committee whom I met at this time and who gave me a strong impression of what they stood for were Colonel John J. McCook, David Murray, Thomas Cochrane, and Cornelius Vanderbilt.[3] I have said some hard

[1] By the time he resigned from the YMCA in April 1898, Eastman had helped organize about forty Indian associations.

[2] Richard C. Morse (1841-1926), a Presbyterian minister, was consulting general secretary of the International Committee of the YMCA (1869-1915). Mott (1865-1955) was general secretary of the International Committee of the YMCA from 1915 to 1931 and general secretary of the National Council of YMCA in the United States until 1928. (Loring) Wilbur Messer (1856-1923) became general secretary of the YMCA in 1888. Charles K. Ober was secretary of the International Committee of the YMCA.

[3] Col. John J. McCook (1845-1911), Civil War soldier and member of the New York law firm of Alexander & Green, served in President William McKinley's first cabinet. During the Spanish-American War in 1898, he became chairman of the Army and

273

things of American Christianity, but in these I referred
to the nation as a whole and to the majority of its people, not to individual Christians. Had I not known
some such, I should long ago have gone back to the
woods.

I wished very much to resume my profession of
medicine, but I was as far as ever from having the capital for a start, and we now had three children. At this
juncture, I was confronted by what seemed a hopeful
opportunity. Some of the leading men of the Sioux,
among them my own brother, Rev. John Eastman,
came to me for a consultation. They argued that I
was the man of their tribe best fitted to look after their
interests in Washington. They had begun to realize
that certain of these interests were of great importance, involving millions of dollars. Although not a
lawyer, they gave me power of attorney to act for them
in behalf of these claims and to appear as their representative before the Indian Bureau, the president, and
Congress.

After signing the necessary papers, I went to Washington, where I urged our rights throughout two ses-

---

Navy Christian Community of the YMCA. A former professor at
Rutgers College (now University), Murray (1830-1905) was advi-
sor to the Imperial Minister of Education of Japan (1873-79). He
also wrote books on Japan, education, and public service. Eastman
may allude to Thomas Cochrane (1871-1936), who was a partner
in the J.P. Morgan & Company and director of Banker's Trust
Company. He was also a trustee of the New York Association for
Improving Conditions of the Poor. Cornelius Vanderbilt III (1873-
1942) was a financier.

John Eastman, Charles Eastman's older brother, 1904

The YMCA building at Pine Ridge Agency

sions and most of a third, while during the summers
I still traveled among the Sioux. I learned that scarcely
one of our treaties with the United States had been
carried out in good faith in all of its provisions. After
the early friendship treaties, which involved no ces-
sion of land, the first was signed in 1824. By this agreement the Sioux gave up a long strip of land lying along
the west bank of the Mississippi, including some of
northern Missouri and eastern Iowa. Out of the pro-
ceeds, we paid several thousand dollars to the Iowa
and Otoe Indians who inhabited this country con-
jointly with us. Next came the treaty ratified in 1837, by
which we parted with all the territory lying in the
southern part of Wisconsin, southeastern Minnesota,
and northeastern Iowa. For this vast domain the government gave us a few thousand dollars in money and
goods, together with many promises, and established
for us a trust fund of $300,000, upon which interest at
5 percent was to be paid "forever." This treaty affected
only certain bands of the Sioux.

In 1851, we ceded another large tract in Iowa and
Minnesota, including some of the best agricultural
lands in the United States, and for this we were to receive ten cents an acre. Two large trust funds were established for the four bands interested, on which
interest at 5 percent was to be paid annually for fifty
years. In addition, the government agreed to furnish
schools, farmers, blacksmith shops, etc., for the civilization of the Sioux. Only nine annual payments had
been made when there was a failure to meet them for

two successive years. Much of our game had disappeared; the people were starving; and this state of affairs, together with various other frauds on the part of government officials and Indian traders, brought on the frightful "Minnesota massacre" in 1862. After this tragedy, many of the Sioux fled into Canada, and the remnant were moved out of state and onto a new reservation in Nebraska. Furthermore, the remaining annuities due them under the treaty were arbitrarily confiscated as a "punishment" for the uprising. It was the claim for these lost annuities, in particular, together with some minor matters, that the Indians now desired to have adjusted, and for which they sent me to the capital.

Now for the first time I seriously studied the machinery of government, and before I knew it, I was a lobbyist. I came to Washington with a great respect for our public men and institutions. Although I had had some disillusioning experiences with the lower type of political henchmen on the reservations, I reasoned that it was because they were almost beyond the pale of civilization and clothed with supreme authority over a helpless and ignorant people that they dared do the things they did. Under the very eye of the law and of society, I thought, this could scarcely be tolerated. I was confident that a fair hearing would be granted and our wrongs corrected without undue delay. I had overmuch faith in the civilized ideal, and I was again disappointed.

I made up my mind at the start that I would keep aloof from the shyster lawyers, and indeed I did not expect to need any legal help until the matter should come before the Court of Claims, which could not be until Congress had acted upon it.

At that time—and I am told that it is much the same now—an Indian could not do business with the department through his attorney. The officials received me courteously enough and assured me that the matters I spoke of should be attended to, but as soon as my back was turned, they pigeonholed them. After waiting patiently, I would resort to the plan of getting one of the Massachusetts senators, who were my friends, to ask for the papers in the case, and this was generally effective. The bureau chiefs soon learned that I had studied our treaty agreements and had some ground for any request that I might make. Naturally enough, every northwestern Indian who came to Washington desired to consult me, and many of them had come on account of personal grievances I could not take up. Complaints of every description came to my ear, not from Indians alone, as some were from earnest white men and women who had served among the Indians and had come up against official graft or abuses. I could not help them much and had to stick pretty closely to my main business.

I was soon haunted and pestered by minor politicians and grafters, each of whom claimed that he was the right-hand man of this or that congressman and that my measure could not pass unless I had the vote of "his" man. Of course, he expected something in exchange for that vote, or rather the promise of it.

Armed with a letter of introduction from one of my staunch eastern senatorial friends, I would approach a legislator who was a stranger to me, in the hope of being allowed to explain to him the purport of our measure. He would listen a while and perhaps refer me to someone else. I would call on the man he named and to my disgust be met with a demand for a liberal percentage on the whole amount to be recovered. If I refused to listen to this proposal, I would soon find the legislator in question "drumming up" some objection to the bill, and these tactics would be kept up until we yielded or made some sort of compromise. My brother John was with me in this work. He is a fine character-reader and would often say to me on leaving someone's office, "Do not trust that man; he is dishonest; he will not keep his word." I found after many months of effort, that political and personal feuds in Congress persistently delayed measures I had looked upon as only common justice.

I appeared from time to time before both House and Senate Committees on Indian Affairs, and a few cases I carried to the president. In this way I have had personal relations with four presidents of the United States, Harrison, Cleveland, McKinley, and Roosevelt.[4] At one time I appeared before the committee

---

[4]These presidents served the following terms: Benjamin Harrison (1833-1901), 1889 to 1893. Grover Cleveland (1837-1908), 1885 to 1889 and 1893 to 1897. William McKinley (b. 1843), 1897 to 1901, when he was assassinated. Theodore Roosevelt (1858-1919), 1901 to 1909.

of which Senator Allison[5] of Iowa was chairman, on the question of allowing the Sisseton Sioux the privilege of leasing their unused allotments to neighboring farmers, without first referring the agreements to the secretary of the interior. The point of the request was that the red tape and long delays greatly handicapped friendly and honest white farmers in their dealings with the Indians, and, as a result, much land lay idle and unbroken.

Someone had circulated a rumor that this measure was fathered by one of the South Dakota senators, with the object of securing some fine Indian lands for his constituents. As soon as I heard of this, I asked for a hearing, which was granted, and I told the committee that this was the Indians' own bill. "We desire to learn business methods," I said, "and we can only do this by handling our own property. You learn by experience to manage your business. How are we Indians to learn if you take from us the wisdom that is born of mistakes and leave us to suffer the stings of robbery and deception, with no opportunity to guard against its recurrence? I know that some will misuse this privilege, and some will be defrauded, but the experiment will be worth all it costs." Instead of asking me further questions upon the bill, they asked: "Where did you go to school? Why are there not more Indians like you?"

[5]Formerly a congressman (1863-71), Sen. William Boyd Allison (1829-1908) represented Iowa from 1873 to 1908.

As I have said, nearly every Indian delegation that came to the capital in those days—and they were many—appealed to me for advice and often had me go over their business with them before presenting it. I was sometimes with them when they had secured their hearing before the Indian commissioner or the committees of Congress, and in this way I heard some interesting speeches. The Ojibways have much valuable pine land, aggregating millions of dollars. Congress had passed an act that authorized a special commissioner to dispose of the lumber for the Indians' benefit, but the new man had not been long in the office when it appeared that he was in with large lumber interests. There was general complaint, but as usual, the Indians were only laughed at, for the official was well-entrenched behind the influence of the lumber kings and of his political party.

At last the Ojibways succeeded in bringing the matter before the House Committee on Indian Affairs, of which James Sherman of New York was chairman.[6] The chief of the delegation addressed the committee somewhat as follows:

"You are very wise men, since to you this great nation entrusts the duty of making laws for the whole people. Because of this, we have trusted you and have hitherto respected the men whom you have sent to manage our affairs. You recently sent one who was

[6]James Schoolcraft Sherman (1855-1912) represented New York in the U.S. Congress from 1887 to 1891, 1893 to 1909. From 1909 to 1912, he was vice president of the United States.

formerly of your number to sell our pines, and he is paid with our money, $10,000 a year. It has been proved that he receives money from the lumber men. He had been underselling all others. We pray you take him away! Every day that you allow him to stay, much money melts away, and great forests fall in thunder!"

Many good speeches lost their effect because of the failure of the uneducated interpreter to render them intelligently, but in this instance a fine linguist interpreted for the chief, the Reverend James Gilfillan, for many years an Episcopal missionary among the Ojibway and well-acquainted with them.

The old men often amused me by their shrewd comments upon our public men. "Old Tom" Beveredge was the Indians' hotelkeeper. They all knew him, and his house was the regular rendezvous. Some Sioux chiefs who had been to call on President Harrison thus characterized him:

Said Young Man Afraid of His Horses: "He is a man of the old trail; he will never make a new one!"

Then American Horse spoke up. "The missionaries tell us that a man cannot have two masters; then how can he be a religious man and a politician at the same time?"

An old chief said of President McKinley: "I never knew a white man to show so much love for mother and wife." "He has a bigger heart than most white men," declared Littlefish, "and this is unfortunate for him. The white man is a man of business and has no use for a heart."

One day, I found a number of the chiefs in the Senate gallery. They observed closely the faces and bearing of the legislators and then gave their verdict. One man they compared to a fish. Another had not the attitude of a true man; that is, held to a pose. Senator Morgan of Alabama they called a great councilor. Senator Hoar they estimated as a patriotic and just statesman. They picked out Senator Platt of Connecticut as being very cautious and a diplomat. They had much difficulty in judging Senator Tillman, but on the whole they considered him to be a fighting man, governed by his emotions rather than his judgment. Some said, he is a loyal friend; others held the reverse. Senator Turpie of Indiana they took for a preacher and were pleased with his air of godliness and reverence. Senator Frye of Maine they thought must be a rarity among white men—honest to the core![7]

It was John Grass who declared that Grover Cleveland was the bravest white chief he had ever known. "The harder you press him," said he, "the stronger he stands."

Theodore Roosevelt has been well-known to the Sioux for over twenty-five years, dating from the years

[7]John Tyler Morgan (1824-1907) was the senator from Alabama from 1877 to 1907. Orville Hitchcock Platt (1827-1905) served as a United States senator from Connecticut from 1879 to 1905. From 1915 to 1929, John Newton Tillman (1859-1929) represented Arkansas in the U.S. Congress. David Turpie (1829-1909) was a U.S. senator from 1887 to 1899. William Pierce Frye (1831-1911) was selected as a U.S. senator in 1881 to fulfill an unexpired term and was re-elected in 1883, serving until his death.

of his ranch life.[8] He was well-liked by them as a rule. Spotted Horse said of him, "While he talked, I forgot that he was a white man."

During Mr. Roosevelt's second administration, there was much disappointment among the Indians. They had cherished hopes of an honest deal, but things seemed to be worse than ever. There were more frauds committed; and in the way of legislation, the Burke bill was distinctly a backward step. The Dawes bill was framed in the interest of the Indians; the Burke bill was for the grafters. Therefore there was much discouragement.[9]

I have been much interested in the point of view of

---

[8]After the death of his wife Alice Hathaway Lee Roosevelt in 1884, Theodore Roosevelt settled on two ranches in the Badlands area of Dakota Territory. By 1886, however, he left the ranch to run for mayor of New York City.

[9]The Dawes Severalty Act or Allotment Act of 1887 allotted tribal lands, then held in common, to individual Indian males and gave citizenship to those who accepted allotment. The goal of the act was to provide Indians with the economic base and education to assimilate into the dominant society. The government opened what it defined as "surplus" land to non-Indian settlement. Eastman and other reform-minded people supported the Dawes Act. Ironically, as a result of the Dawes Act, Native Americans lost in the next fifty years more than 85 million acres. Charles Burke, a South Dakota Republican congressman and chair of the House Committee on Indian Affairs, subsequently sponsored the Burke Act (1906), an amendment to the Dawes Act. This legislation dealt with Indian allotment fees, patents, and citizenship. Reformers like Eastman particularly opposed its provisions that made it more difficult for Indians to acquire citizenship. Eastman argued that its framers were interested only in graft and believed the law would confuse the status of the Indians.

these older Indians. Our younger element has now been so thoroughly drilled in the motives and methods of the white man, at the same time losing the old mother and family training through being placed in boarding school from six years of age onward, that they have really become an entirely different race.

During this phase of my life, I was brought face-to-face with a new phase of progress among my people of the Dakotas. Several of their reservations were allotted in severalty, and the Indians became full citizens and voters. As the population of these new states was still small and scattered, the new voters, although few in number, were of distinct interest to the candidates for office, and their favor was eagerly sought. In some counties, the Indian vote held the balance of power.

At first they continued to get together according to old custom, calling a council and giving a preliminary feast, at which two or three steers would be killed for a barbecue. After dinner, the tribal herald called the men together to hear the candidate or his representative. I took active part in one or two campaigns, but they have now a number of able young men who expound politics to them locally.

Some persons imagine that we are still wild savages, living on the hunt or on rations; but as a matter of fact, we Sioux are now fully entrenched, for all practical purposes, in the warfare of civilized life.

XXIII

Back to the Woods

IN THE SUMMER of 1910, I accepted a commission to search out and purchase rare curios and ethnological specimens for one of the most important collections in the country.[1] Very few genuine antiques are now to be found among Indians living on reservations, and the wilder and more scattered bands who still treasure them cannot easily be induced to give them up. My method was one of indirection. I would visit for several days in a camp where I knew, or had reason to believe, that some of the coveted articles were to be found. After I had talked much with the leading men, feasted with them, and made them presents, a slight hint would often result in the chief or medicine man "presenting" me with some object of historic or ceremonial interest, which etiquette would not permit to be "sold" and which a white man would probably not have been allowed to see at all.

I know of no Indians within the borders of the United States, except those of Leech, Cass, and Red Lakes in Minnesota,[2] who still sustain themselves after

[1]In 1910, Eastman was collecting Native American artifacts for the University of Pennsylvania Museum.
[2]Leech, Cass, and Red Lakes were reservations in northern Minnesota.

the old fashion by hunting, fishing, and the gathering of wild rice and berries. They do, to be sure, have a trifle of annuity money from the sale of their pinelands, and now and then they sell a few trinkets. Their permanent houses are of logs or frame, but they really do not live in them except during the coldest part of the year. Even then, some of them may be found far away from their villages, trapping for furs, which may still be disposed of at convenient points along the Canadian border. They travel by canoe or on foot, as they own very few horses and there are no roads through the forest—only narrow trails, deeply grooved in the virgin soil.

The Leech Lake Ojibways, to whom I made my first visit, appear perfectly contented and irresponsible. They have plenty to eat of the choicest wild game, wild rice, and berries. The making of maple sugar is a leading industry. The largest band and by far the most interesting is that which inhabits Bear Island. The group plants no gardens, will have nothing to do with school or churches, and meets annually, as of old, for the Grand Medicine Dance, or sacred festival, invoking the protection and blessing of the Great Mystery for the year to come.

I am a Sioux, and the Ojibways were once the fiercest of our enemies, yet I was kindly welcomed by the principal chief, Majigabo, who even permitted me to witness the old rites upon their "sacred ground." This particular spot, they told me, had been in use for more than forty years, and the moose-hide drum, stretched upon a cylinder of basswood, was fully as venerable. The dance hall was about a hundred feet long, roofed with poles and thatch. In the center was a rude altar, and the entrance faced the rising sun. While the ceremonies went on, groups of young men were sitting in the shade and gambling with primitive dice—small carved bones shaken in a polished bowl of bird's-eye maple.

Majigabo is one of the few Indians left alive who ventured to defy a great government with a handful of savages. Only a few years ago, Captain Wilkinson was shot down at the head of his troop, while advancing to frighten the Bear Islanders into obedience. The trouble originated in the illegal sale of whiskey to the Indians. One of the tribesmen was summoned to Duluth as a witness and at the close of the trial turned loose to walk home, a distance of over a hundred miles. The weather was severe, and he reached his people half-starved and sick from exposure. The next time one was summoned, he not unnaturally refused to appear. After the death of Captain Wilkinson, no further attempt was made at coercion.

"They can take everything else, but they must let me and these island people alone," the chief said to me, and I could not but sympathize with his attitude. Only last spring he refused to allow the census taker to enumerate his people.

The next man I went to see was Boggimogishig. The old war chief of the Sugar Point band was one of those who most frequently went against the Eastern

Sioux and was often successful. This good fortune was attributed largely to the influence of the sacred war club, which had been handed down through several generations of dauntless leaders. I made use of the old-time Indian etiquette, as well as of all the wit and humor at my command, to win a welcome, and finally obtained from the old man the history and traditions of his people, so far as he knew them, and even the famous war club itself!

At Red Lake, I found the men just returned from a successful moose hunt, and although they greeted me kindly, it appeared that some of the older warriors, recalling hand-to-hand scrimmages with my forbears, were somewhat embarrassed by the presence of a Sioux visitor. However, after I had been properly introduced and had conformed with the good old customs relating to intertribal meetings, I secured several things that I had come in search of, and among them some very old stories. It appears that a battle was once fought between Ojibways and Sioux near the mouth of the stream called Battle Creek. While the waters of the stream ran with blood, the color was even discernible upon the shores of the lake, which has ever since been known as Red Lake. It was this battle, indeed, that finally decided the question of occupancy. For it is said that although my people succeeded for the time in holding off the Ojibways and cast many of the bodies of their dead enemies into the river, they lost so heavily themselves and became so disheartened that they then left forever behind them their life

Charles Eastman at Lake Minnetonka, New York, 1927

Charles Eastman with a guide and bark canoe on Rainy Lake, Ontario

From the Deep Woods to Civilization

in the forest. They exchanged the canoe and birch-bark tepee for the prairie and the buffalo.

But it is on Rainy Lake, remote and solitary, and still further to the north and west upon the equally lovely Lake of the Woods, that I found the true virgin wilderness, the final refuge, as it appears, of American big game and primitive man. The international line at this point is formed by the Rainy River, lying deep in its rocky bed and connecting the two lakes, both of which are adorned with thousands of exquisite islands of a gemlike freshness and beauty. The clear, black waters have washed, ground, and polished these rocky islets into every imaginable fantastic shape, and all are carpeted with velvety mosses in every shade of gray and green, and canopied with fairylike verdure. In every direction one is beckoned by vistas of extraordinary charm.

These aboriginal woodsmen are in type quite distinct from the Plains Indians. They are generally tall and well-proportioned, of somewhat lighter complexion than their brethren to the southward, and very grave and reticent. Their homes and food are practically those of two centuries ago, the only change observable being that the inconvenient blanket is for the most part discarded and the men carry guns instead of bows and arrows.

It was in the middle of August, the time for tying into bundles the wild rice straw, in the great bays where nature has so plentifully sown it. To each family belong its sheaves, and when the tying is finished, they are apt to linger in the neighborhood, the women making sacks while the men hunt. A month later comes the harvest. Two by two they go out in canoes, one to paddle, while the other seizes the bundle of rice straw and strikes a few smart blows with a stick. The ripe grain rattles into the canoe, which, when half full, is emptied on shore, and so on until the watery fields are cleared.

I had now to follow these family groups to their hidden resorts, and the sweet roving instinct of the wild took forcible hold upon me once more. I was eager to realize for a few perfect days the old, wild life as I knew it in my boyhood, and I set out with an Ojibway guide in his birch canoe, taking with me little that belonged to the white man, except his guns, fishing tackle, knives, and tobacco. The guide carried some Indian-made maple sugar and a sack of wild rice, a packet of black tea and a kettle, and we had a blanket apiece. Only think of pitching your tent upon a new island every day in the year! Upon many a little rocky terrace, shaded by pine and cedar trees, hard by a tiny harbor with its fleet of birchen canoes, the frail bark lodges stood about in groups, looking as if they had grown there. Before each lodge there is a fireplace, and near at hand the women of the family may often be seen making nets and baskets, or cooking the simple meal.

Early in the summer mornings there is a pleasant stir in the camp, when they glide in canoes over the placid waters, lifting their nets full of glistening fish.

Perhaps the sturgeon net is successful; then laughter and whoops of excitement break the stillness, for the king of the lake fights for his life and pulls the boat about vigorously before he is finally knocked on the head and towed into camp.

Up on Seine Bay the favorite sport was hunting the loon, which scarcely ever takes to the wing but dives on being approached. Most people would be put to it to guess in which direction he would reappear, at a distance of from a quarter-mile to half a mile, but these sons of nature have learned his secret. As soon as he goes under, the canoes race for a certain point, and invariably the bird comes up among them. He is greeted with derisive laughter and cheers, and immediately dives again, and the maneuver is repeated until he is winded and caught. The flesh of the loon has a strong, fishy flavor, but these Indians are very fond of it. With them nothing goes to waste. All meat or fish not needed for immediate use is cut into thin strips and smoked or dried. The hoofs of deer and moose are made into trinkets, the horns into spoons or tobacco boards, and the bones pounded to boil out the fat, which is preserved in dried bladders or bags of pelican skin.

At North Bay I heard of a remarkable old woman, said to be well over ninety years of age, the daughter of a longtime chief during the good old days. I called at her solitary birchbark tepee and found her out, but she soon returned bent under a load of bark for making mats, with roots and willow twigs for dye. She was persuaded to sit for her picture and even to tell some old stories of her people, which she did with much vivacity. There are less than a hundred of them left!

The name given to this ancient crone by the lumberjacks is shockingly irreverent. It is told that when she was a handsome young woman, her father, the ruling chief, was honored by the Hudson Bay Company. More than one of its employees came courting after the fashion of those days. But the daughter of the woods could not endure the sight of a white man, with his repulsive hairy face. It seems that one day, when she was approached by a bearded voyageur, she screamed and raised her knife, so that the man fled, cursing her. Thereafter, whenever she saw a white man, she would innocently repeat this oath, until she came to be known among them by that name.

As we wound in and out of the island labyrinth, new beauties met us at every turn. At one time there were not less than eight moose in sight, and the deer were plentiful and fearless. As we glided through the water, the Ojibway repeated in his broken dialect some of their traditions. We passed "Massacre Island," where, more than a hundred years ago, some French traders are said to have brought the "firewater" to a large village of innocent natives, thinking thus to buy their furs for a trifle. But the Indians, when crazed with liquor, rose up and killed them all instead, even a Catholic priest who was unfortunately of the party. Since that day, the spirit of the "Black Robe,"

who died praying, is believed to haunt the deserted island, and no Indian ever sets foot there.

Every day it became harder for me to leave the
woods. Finally I took passage on a gasoline launch
that plied between a lumber camp and the little city of
International Falls. The air had been dense with
smoke all day because of immense forest fires on both
sides of the lake. As it grew dark, we entered a narrow
channel between the islands, when the wind suddenly
rose, and the pilot feared lest we should be blown
from the only known course, for much of the lake is
not charted. He swung about for the nearest islands,
a cluster of three, knowing that only on one side of
these was it possible to land. It was dark as pitch and
raining hard when we were struck broadside by a
heavy wave; the windows were knocked out and all
the lights extinguished.

There was nothing to do but jump and swim for it,
and it seems almost a miracle that we all landed safely.
There were just four of us playing Robinson Crusoe
on a lively little isle of about an acre in extent—too
small to harbor any game. The boat was gone with all
its freight, except a few things that drifted ashore.
Here we remained for two nights and a day before we
were discovered.

This accident delayed me a day or two, as I had to
buy another canoe and provisions for my last plunge
into the wilderness. It carried me up Seine Bay and
into the Seine River. One day we came unexpectedly
upon a little Indian village of neatly made bark houses

in a perfect state of preservation, but to my surprise it was uninhabited. What was still stranger, I found that whoever lived there had left all their goods behind, dishes, clothing, even bundles of furs all moth-eaten and ruined. We reached there late in the afternoon, and I immediately decided to stay the night. After supper, the guide told me that a band of Indians had lived here every winter for several years, hunting for the Hudson Bay Company. One winter, many of their children were attacked by an unknown disease. After several had died, the people fled in terror, leaving everything behind them. This happened, he said, eleven years before. While he was talking, beside the fire we had built in the rude mud chimney of one of the deserted cabins, in the perfectly still night, it all seemed weird and mysterious. Suddenly we heard a loud scratching on the bark door, as if some hand were feeling for the latch. He stopped speaking and we looked at one another. The scratching was repeated. "Shall I open the door?" I said. I had my hand on the trigger of my Smith and Wesson. He put more sticks on the fire. When I got the door open, there stood the biggest turtle I have ever seen, raised upon his hind feet, his eyes shining, his tail defiantly lifted, as if to tell us that he was at home and we were the intruders.

XXIV

The Soul of the White Man

MY LAST work under the auspices of the government was the revision of the Sioux allotment
rolls, including the determination of family groups
and the assignment of surnames when these were
lacking.[1] Originally, the Indians had no family names,
and confusion has been worse confounded by the
admission to the official rolls of vulgar nicknames,
incorrect translations, and English cognomens inju-
diciously bestowed upon children in various schools.
Mr. Hamlin Garland and Dr. George Bird Grinnell
interested themselves in this matter some years ago,[2]
and President Roosevelt foresaw the difficulties and

[1]From 1903 to 1909, Eastman worked on revising the names of
approximately 25,000 to 30,000 Sioux.

[2]Hamlin Garland (1860-1940) was a novelist and short-story
writer. Partly raised in Dakota Territory, Garland is best known for
his fiction about the West. Garland, who was a strong believer in
reform of federal policies on Indians, advocated abolishing the allotment system and encouraging American Indian art and religion. Convinced that Native Americans must have proper last
names if they were to avoid legal difficulties as landowners, he
strongly supported the renaming project. In 1902, Garland wrote
a circular outlining procedures to be followed in the renaming
project. The Indian Bureau issued the circular. Garland is also
the author of *The Book of the American Indian* (1923). He recruited Grinnell to support the renaming of Indians. Dr. George
Bird Grinnell (1849-1938) received his Ph.D. in zoology and in

complications in the way of land inheritance, hence my unique commission.

My method was to select from the personal names of a family one which should be reasonably short, euphonious, and easily pronounced by the white man in the vernacular, or, failing this, a short translation in which the essential meaning should be preserved. All the brothers, their wives and children were then grouped under this as a family name, provided their consent could be obtained to the arrangement.

While fully appreciating the Indian's viewpoint, I have tried to convince him of the sincerity of his white friends but that conflicts between the two races have been due to the selfish greed of some white men. These children of nature once had faith in man as well as in God. Today, they would suspect even their best friend. A "century of dishonor" and abuse of their trust has brought them to this. Accordingly, it was rumored among them that the revision of names was another cunning scheme of the white man to defraud them of the little land still left in their possession. The older men would sit in my office and watch my work day after day before being convinced that the undertaking was really intended for their benefit and that of their heirs. Once satisfied, they were of great assistance, for some of them knew by heart the family tree

---

1874 served as the naturalist on Custer's expedition in the Black Hills. An anthropologist and historian as well, he wrote highly praised books on the Cheyenne and collections of oral literature from the Cheyenne, Pawnee, and Blackfeet.

of nearly every Indian in that particular band for four generations. Their memories are remarkable, and many a fact of historic interest came up in the course of our discussions.

Such names as "Young Man of Whose Horses the Enemy Is Afraid," "He Kills Them on Horseback," and the like, while highly regarded among us, are not easily rendered into English nor pronounced in the Dakota. Aside from such troubles, I had many difficulties with questionable marriages and orphaned children whose ancestry was not clear. Then there were cases of Indian women who had married United States soldiers, and the children who had been taken away from the tribe in infancy but later returned as young men and women to claim their rights.

I was directed not to recognize a plurality of wives, such as still existed among a few of the older men. Old White Bull was a fine example of the old type, and I well remember his answer when I reluctantly informed him that each man must choose one wife who should bear his name. "What!" he exclaimed. "These two women are sisters, both of whom have been my wives for over half a century. I know the way of the white man; he takes women unknown to each other and to his law. These two have been faithful to me, and I have been faithful to them. Their children are my children, and their grandchildren are mine. We are now living together as brother and sisters. All the people know that we have been happy together, and nothing but death can separate us."

This work occupied me for six years and gave me insight into the relationships and intimate history of 30,000 Sioux.

My first book, *Indian Boyhood*, embodying the recollections of my wild life, appeared in 1902, and the favor with which it was received has encouraged me to attempt a fuller expression of our people's life from the inside. The present is the eighth that I have done, always with the devoted cooperation of my wife. Although but one book, *Wigwam Evenings*, bears both our names, we have worked together, she in the little leisure remaining to the mother of six children, and I in the intervals of lecturing and other employment. For the past twelve years our home has been in a New England college town,[3] and our greatest personal concern the upbringing and education of our children.

None of my earlier friends who knew me well would ever have believed that I was destined to appear in the role of a public speaker! It may be that I shared the native gift of oratory in some degree, but I had also the Indian reticence with strangers. Perhaps the one man most responsible for this phase of my work, aside from circumstances, was Major James B. Pond of New York City, the famous lyceum manager.[4] Soon after the publication of *Indian Boyhood*, I came from

[3]They lived in Amherst, Massachusetts, home of Amherst College.

[4]Maj. James Burton Pond of New York City (1838-1903) owned the Lyceum Lecture Bureau, located in New York City. After Pond died, Elaine Goodale Eastman managed her husband's lecture engagements.

South Dakota to Brooklyn by invitation of the Twentieth Century Club of that city, to address them on the Indian. Major Pond heard of this and invited me to luncheon. He had my book with him, and after a good deal of talk, he persuaded me to go on the lecture platform under his management. He took the most cordial interest in the matter and prepared the copy of my first circular. His untimely death during the next summer put a damper upon my beginning; nevertheless, I filled all the dates he had made for me, and finding a growing demand, I have continued in the field ever since.

My chief object has been not to entertain but to present the American Indian in his true character before Americans. The barbarous and atrocious character commonly attributed to him has dated from the transition period, when the strong drink, powerful temptations, and commercialism of the white man led to deep demoralization. Really it was a campaign of education on the Indian and his true place in American history.

I have been, on the whole, happily surprised to meet with so cordial a response. Again and again I have been told by recognized thinkers, "You present an entirely new viewpoint. We can never again think of the Indian as we have done before." A great psychologist wrote me after reading *The Soul of the Indian*: "My God! why did we not know these things sooner?" Many of my hearers have admitted that morality and spirituality are found to thrive better under the simplest conditions than in a highly organized society and that the virtues are more readily cultivated where the "struggle for existence" is merely a struggle with the forces of nature, and not with one's fellow men.

The philosophy of the original American was to demonstrate on a high plane, that his gift of eloquence, wit, humor, and poetry is well established; his democracy and community life was much nearer the ideal than ours today; his standard of honor and friendship unsurpassed; and all his faults are the faults of generous youth.

It was not until I felt that I had to a degree established these claims that I consented to appear on the platform in our ancestral garb of honor. I feel that I was a pioneer in this new line of defense of the Native American, not so much of his rights in the land as of his character and religion. I am glad that the drift is now toward a better understanding and that he is become the acknowledged hero of the Boy Scouts and Camp Fire Girls, as well as of many artists, sculptors, and sincere writers.

I was invited to represent the North American Indian at the First Universal Races Congress in London, England, in 1911. It was a great privilege to attend that gathering of distinguished representatives of fifty-three different nationalities, come together to mutually acquaint themselves with one another's progress and racial ideals. I was entertained by some well-known men, but there was little time for purely social enjoyment. What impressed me most was the perfect equality of the races, which formed the background of all the discussions. It was declared at the outset that there is no superior race, and no inferior, since individuals of all races have proved their innate capacity by their standing in the universities of the world, and it has not seldom happened that men of the undeveloped races have surpassed students of the most advanced races in scholarship and ability.

One little incident caused some of the delegates of the Asiatic peoples to approach me with a special friendliness. I was at a committee meeting where the platform of the Congress was being drafted, and as the first paragraph was read, I noticed that the word "Christian" appeared several times. I rose and said, "While I am myself a believer in the simple principles of Christianity, we who are met here are not all of that religion, and I would suggest that we substitute a term to which we can all subscribe, since we meet here not in the name but in the spirit of Christianity, of universal brotherhood." Several sprang up to second the motion, among them Mr. John Milholland and Dr. Felix Adler, and as I saw Mr. Edwin D. Mead of Boston near by, I began to feel more at home.[5] I was invited by some

---

[5]John Elmer Milholland (1860-1925), a writer for the *New York Tribune* and businessman, advocated constitutional rights for African Americans, prison reform, and federal aid to education. He was also active in the First Races Congress, London, 1911. Adler (1851-1933) was a professor of Hebrew at Cornell University and later a professor of political and social science at Columbia

Oriental representatives present to visit them in their own country, but as I was tied up with Chautauqua engagements,[6] I had to take the next boat for home.

A very pleasant occasion of my meeting men and women distinguished in literature was the banquet given to Mark Twain on his seventieth birthday.[7] Another interesting meeting was the dinner given by the Rocky Mountain Club of New York to fifteen western governors. I believe I was the only speaker there who was not a governor.

It has been my privilege to visit nearly all sections of our country on lecture tours, including semitropical Florida and the Pacific coast, the great prairie states, and almost every nook and corner of picturesque New England. I have been entertained at most of our great colleges and universities, from coast

---

University. He founded the Society for Ethnical Culture in 1876. Edwin Doak Mead (1849-1937), author and lecturer, edited *New England Magazine* and the *International Library*. He was director of the World Peace Foundation and a delegate of the American Peace Society to Peace Congresses in Europe.

[6]The chautauquas began in 1874 as secular as well as religious assemblies at Fair Point (later called Chautauqua), New York. Later chautauquas quickly expanded their programs to cover education and include popular entertainments. After the chautauqua concept spread to many communities throughout the country, a circuit chautauqua plan emerged in 1904. Many distinguished men and women appeared at these assemblies.

[7]Born 30 November 1835, Samuel Clemens, known as Mark Twain, became one of America's most popular writers. His seventieth anniversary dinner was held on 5 December 1905, at the fashionable Delmonico's in New York City. He died in 1910.

to coast, and had the honor of acquaintance with many famous and interesting people, among whom I might name almost at random, W.D. Howells, Hamlin Garland, Ernest Thompson Seton,[8] Dr. George Bird Grinnell, authors; Lorado Taft, sculptor[9] (at the unveiling of whose colossal *Black Hawk* I was privileged to officiate); Edwin W. Deming, Ernest Blumenschein, and other noted artists; Mme. Bloomfield Zeisler, pianist; John Hays Hammond, engineer;[10] presidents G. Stanley Hall, Ernest Fox Nichols, Eliot, Stryker, Harry Pratt Judson, Dr. Luther Gulick, and other noted educators;[11] Rabbi Stephen S. Wise,

[8]William Dean Howells (1837-1920) was an American novelist, critic, and editor. An animal painter, lecturer, and prolific author of books on animals and natural history, Ernest Thompson Seton (1860-1946) founded both the Boy Scout movement in America and the Woodcraft League of America. He highly respected Eastman. Seton's books include *The Gospel of the Red Man: An Indian Bible* (1936).

[9]Lorado Taft (1860-1936) was a sculptor, lecturer, and teacher. In 1912, he created the huge statue called *Black Hawk*, located in Oregon, Illinois.

[10]Edwin W. Deming (1860-1942), an artist and illustrator, painted Indian and animal subjects; he illustrated the Eastmans' *Wigwam Evenings:Sioux Folk Tales Retold* (1919).Ernest L. Blumenschein (b. 1874) was an illustrator for many magazines and a portrait painter; he illustrated *Indian Boyhood* (1902). Fannie Bloomfield Zeisler (1863-1927), acclaimed as one of the world's great concert pianists, emigrated with her family from Austria to the United States in 1867, settling in Chicago in 1869. She married Sigmund Zeisler in 1885. John Hays Hammond (1855-1936) gained international recognition as a mining engineer and as a businessman affiliated with financial groups that purchased and promoted mining properties in the United States and Mexico.

[11]G(ranville) Stanley Hall (1844-1924) was a psychologist and

several bishops, and prominent clergymen of all denominations, together with a large circle not so well known to the public but whose society has been to me equally stimulating and delightful.

Like everyone else who is more or less in the public eye, I have a large correspondence from unknown friends. Among the most inspiring letters received have been those from foreign countries, where, until the outbreak of the European war, I had not only generous critics, but translators of my books in France, Germany, Austria, Bohemia, and Denmark. I am frequently asked to recommend to readers books on all phases of Indian life and art, also to criticize such books both in print and in manuscript.

My work for the Boy Scouts, whose program appeals to me strongly, has given me a good deal of practice in camp management.[12] That finally guided me to

---

president of Clark College (now University), Worcester, Massachusetts (1889-1920). A physicist, Ernest Fox Nichols (1869-1924) was president of Dartmouth College (1909-16) and of Massachusetts Institute of Technology (1921).Charles William Eliot (1834-1926) was an educator and president of Harvard from 1869 to 1909. Melancthon Woolsey Stryker (1851-1929), theologian and hymnologist, was president of Hamilton College, Clinton, New York (1892-1917). Harry Pratt Judson (1849-1927), a political scientist, was acting president (1906-1907) and president (1907-23) of the University of Chicago. Luther H. Gulick (1865-1918), a medical doctor and educator, was director of physical training of the New York City public schools (1903-1909) and president of the Camp Fire Girls (1913). He authored many books on health and physical education.

[12]Eastman began his work with the Boy Scouts in 1910.

Charles Eastman during a visit to Dartmouth College

Courtesy Dartmouth College Library

309

Charles Eastman, in the 1920s

Courtesy Dartmouth College Library

Charles Eastman teaching archery at the
summer camp operated by the Eastmans

From the Deep Woods to Civilization

organizing summer camps for both boys and girls on
charming Granite Lake in the hills of southern New
Hampshire, where my whole family are enthusiastic
helpers in the development of this form of open-air
education, which is patterned largely upon my own
early training.[13]

From the time I first accepted the Christ ideal, it
has grown upon me steadily, but I also see more and
more plainly our modern divergence from that ideal.
I confess I have wondered much that Christianity is
not practiced by the very people who vouch for that
wonderful conception of exemplary living. It appears
that they are anxious to pass on their religion to all
races of men but keep very little of it themselves. I
have not seen the meek inherit the earth, or the peace-
makers receive high honor.

Why do we find so much evil and wickedness practiced by the nations composed of professedly "Christian" individuals? The pages of history are full of
licensed murder and the plundering of weaker and
less-developed peoples, and obviously the world
today has not outgrown this system. Behind the material and intellectual splendor of our civilization,
primitive savagery and cruelty and lust hold sway,
undiminished, and as it seems, unheeded. When I let

[13]In 1915, the Eastmans opened their summer camp for girls,
School of the Woods, located at Granite Lake, near Munsonville,
New Hampshire. The whole family worked at the camp. The next
year, they included boys, changing the name to Camp Oahe for
girls and Camp Ohiyesa for boys.

go of my simple, instinctive nature religion, I hoped to gain something far loftier as well as more satisfying. Alas! it is also more confusing and contradictory. The higher and spiritual life, though first in theory, is clearly secondary, if not entirely neglected, in actual practice. When I reduce civilization to its lowest terms, it becomes a system of life based upon trade. The dollar is the measure of value, and *might* still spells *right*; otherwise, why war?

Yet even in deep jungles God's own sunlight penetrates, and I stand before my own people still as an advocate of civilization. Why? First, because there is no chance for our former simple life anymore; and second, because I realize that the white man's religion is not responsible for his mistakes. There is every evidence that God has given him all the light necessary by which to live in peace and goodwill with his brother; and we also know that many brilliant civilizations have collapsed in physical and moral decadence. It is for us to avoid their fate if we can.

I am an Indian; and while I have learned much from civilization, for which I am grateful, I have never lost my Indian sense of right and justice. I am for development and progress along social and spiritual lines, rather than those of commerce, nationalism, or material efficiency. Nevertheless, so long as I live, I am an American.

Index

INDEX

List of The Lakeside Classics

The Lakeside Classics

DESIGNED, TYPESET, PRINTED, BOUND, AND DISTRIBUTED BY
R.R. DONNELLEY & SONS COMPANY

COMPOSITION:
ALLENTOWN DIGITAL SERVICES,
ALLENTOWN, PENNSYLVANIA

SCANNING, COMPUTER TO PLATES, PRESSWORK, AND BINDING:
CRAWFORDSVILLE, INDIANA, BOOK MANUFACTURING DIVISION

IMAGE PROOFING (KODAK APPROVAL XP4):
LANCASTER, PENNSYLVANIA, PREMEDIA CENTER,
NORTHEAST DIVISION

WORLDWIDE DISTRIBUTION:
DONNELLEY LOGISTICS SERVICES

E-BOOK VERSION:
HTML CONVERSION, ALLENTOWN DIGITAL SERVICES
SITE MAINTENANCE, TECHNOLOGY CENTER,
DOWNERS GROVE, ILLINOIS
www.rrdonnelley.com/elakeside

BODY TYPEFACE:
11/12 POINT BULMER

PAPER STOCK:
50-POUND WHITE LAKESIDE CLASSICS OPAQUE,
50-PERCENT RECYCLED SHEET, BY GLATFELTER

CLOTH:
ROXITE C VELLUM CHOCOLATE BROWN,
BY HOLLISTON MILLS, INC.